DENNY MATTHEWS'S
TALES FROM THE

ROYALS

—— DUGOUT ——

Denny Matthews
with
Matt Fulks

Foreword by Frank White

SportsPublishingLLC.com

Publishers: Peter L. Bannon and Joseph J. Bannon Sr.
Senior managing editor: Susan M. Moyer
Acquisitions editor: Bob Snodgrass
Developmental editor: Doug Hoepker
Art director: K. Jeffrey Higgerson
Dust jacket design: Kenneth J. O'Brien
Interior layout: Kenneth J. O'Brien
Imaging: Kenneth J. O'Brien
Photo editor: Erin Linden-Levy

Printed in the United States of America

Sports Publishing L.L.C.
804 North Neil Street
Champaign, IL 61820

Phone: 1-877-424-2665
Fax: 217-363-2073
SportsPublishingLLC.com

Library of Congress Cataloging-in-Publication Data

Matthews, Denny, 1942-
    Denny Matthews's tales from the Royals dugout / Denny Matthews with Matt Fulks ; foreword by Frank White.
        p. cm.
    ISBN 1-59670-039-4 (softcover : alk. paper)
    1. Kansas City Royals (Baseball team)—Anecdotes. 2. Kansas City Royals (Baseball team)—History. I. Fulks, Matt. II. Title.

GV875.K3M38 2006
796.357'6409778411—dc22

                              2006001203

This book is dedicated to all the past and present men who have worn Royal blue. In particular, we remember the great Royals who are no longer with us, including Ewing and Muriel Kauffman, Joe Burke, Dick Howser, Al Cowens, Darrell Porter, and Dan Quisenberry. You will always be remembered.

CONTENTS

Foreword

By Frank White,
Five-Time All-Star and World Series Champion

Do you ever sit and wonder what your life would be like if it hadn't been for one major event? I sometimes do. That one event for me was being selected for the Royals Baseball Academy. The academy was an experimental brainchild of former Kansas City Royals owner Ewing Kauffman, who thought that the Royals could find good athletes and turn them into major-league caliber baseball players.

After a successful tryout in 1970, at the age of 19, I was selected by the Royals for the academy. Even though I could play baseball, I wasn't a major-league prospect. My high school, Lincoln High in Kansas City, didn't have a baseball team, so my playing was confined to summer leagues, including Kansas City's Ban Johnson League. In fact, when I tried out for the academy, I was a sheet metal clerk at Metals Protection Plating Company. Certainly not a place to be seen by big-league scouts.

The academy's director, Syd Thrift, believed in me, though. One of the team's main rules was that players were not to be married. Guess what? I was married. But Syd convinced Mr. Kauffman that I should be a part of the academy.

During our time at the Royals Baseball Academy in Florida, we weren't allowed to have cars, we stayed in dormitories, we went to Manatee Junior College for classes, and then we spent hours each day working on the fundamentals of baseball. Professionally, it was one of the best things that could have happened to me.

Less than three years later, in 1973, I returned to Kansas City as a member of the Royals. It was a dream come true. I often have said that my greatest thrill as a baseball player, by far, was being called to the major leagues and playing for my hometown Royals.

Playing in two World Series, including the 1985 championship, is an unbelievable feeling. But to be able to play at a high level for so long in front of family and friends in my hometown is hard to beat. To do that for nearly 20 years is rare.

Now, to see my No. 20 at the bottom of the scoreboard, along with the numbers of my teammate George Brett and manager Dick Howser, and to think that I was the only hometown player to spend his entire career with the club, is humbling beyond words.

Even though there was a time, in 1984, when I asked to be traded, it's hard to imagine playing anywhere except in my hometown and its great fans. Ironically, if it hadn't been for Mr. Kauffman, not only would I not have had a chance to play major league baseball, but major league baseball might not have been in Kansas City during the 1970s.

There was a period, after the Kansas City A's left and went to Oakland, when we had a feeling in Kansas City that we'd never have baseball again. At the urging of several business leaders in the area, though, Mr. Kauffman stepped up and bought the team.

When the Royals started playing in 1969, all of us were hooked. I wanted to listen to the games or watch them in person as much as I could.

Lincoln High School was situated right next to the old Municipal Stadium, the Royals' first home. The school sat on a hill, which allowed us to stand on the bleachers at the football field and look down into Municipal Stadium and watch games. It was great when I had a gym class at 1:00 in the afternoon on days when the Royals would be playing an afternoon game. I was in baseball heaven.

When the Royals played at night, we'd climb up to the top of the bleachers after baseball practice and watch the game until about the sixth or seventh inning. Then, late in the game, we would go down to the left field bleachers where George Toma, the team's groundskeeper, would open the gates and let us sneak in to watch the last couple innings. Again, what an experience!

It was cool to watch the Royals players leave after the game and to imagine being one of them one day. We looked at those guys as heroes. It's funny, because a few years later, I was playing with many of those same players.

When I wasn't sneaking a peek at Municipal, or making the short trip to the stadium with my dad, I was listening on the radio. I loved listening to Buddy Blattner and Denny Matthews. As the veteran announcer, Buddy put you in the ballpark; he made you think you were there. That's what you want when you're at home listening to the game. Buddy created an atmosphere. Today's younger announcers aren't like that.

Denny learned quite a bit from Buddy. Denny has been able to sustain, which is obvious by the fact that he's been with the Royals since day one. When it comes to the action on the field, Denny is about as knowledgeable as they come. He grew up playing the game, but he's also studied it. There often are times when he'll sit down with a player and talk about the position, or learn the player's thoughts on different situations. I know, because he and I have had a few discussions about second base play.

Through Denny's knowledge of the game, and his memory throughout the club's history, in *Tales from the Royals Dugout*, he and Matt Fulks spin some fantastic stories and insight into some of the people who have shaped the history of this organization.

The book brought back some fantastic memories for me, such as the series against the A's in Oakland in 1976 when we had a fight one night and then came back the next night and clinched a share of our first American League Western division championship behind a heroic game from Amos Otis and some terrific managing by Whitey Herzog.

I played for Whitey at a young age. Most of our club was young when Whitey managed us. He was a great young player's manager. He was an aggressive manager who liked all-out play from all of his guys. He basically let us play. He taught us to trust ourselves as players, go out and play the game the same way regardless of the situation, and then he'd take over in the seventh inning if needed.

He wanted us to use good judgment. He let us put on our own hit-and-runs and our own steals. As long as we made good decisions, he wasn't going to give us a hard time. I think that's what we needed at that time. He was a great manager to play for.

Tales from the Royals Dugout also brought back some hilarious memories of Big John Mayberry sitting in the back of the bus, needling guys in a way that only Big John could do.

And, of course, Denny recalls some stories from our World Series championship season of 1985, when I became the second second baseman in history—after Jackie Robinson—to bat cleanup in the Series, thanks to my favorite manager, Dick Howser.

Dick saw that I could be both a good defensive player and a productive offensive player, which no other manager seemed to see. From 1983 to '87, Dick batted me in run-producing positions. During that span when he moved me to the third spot, I had 17, 22, 22, and 17 home runs. My production went down after 1987 when I was moved down in the order. Dick saw a complete player in me, for which I'll always be grateful.

Dick was a true professional. He had been with the Yankees, a club that didn't mess much with young guys. From my standpoint from day one, in 1981, he knew how to handle veteran players, which is what we needed at that time. Through his faith in us and our desire to win for him, we had a magical season in 1985.

Winning that World Series was an incredible experience. I feel especially blessed because we missed several opportunities in the 1970s, and then we were close in 1980. So to be a part of the club's first world championship, and to be a part of that with a team from my hometown, is special. Seeing the excitement of the fans in 1980 and 1985 was a big thrill. We all were experiencing some incredible moments.

Our teams played well and had fun all those years because we had good players. Having the chemistry and becoming winners came from having good players. We held each other accountable for what happened on the field. We weren't going to get the other team tomorrow; we were going to get them that day. We wanted to win that day, every day. That was the backbone of our success. We had talented players and a strong desire as a team to win.

People often want to mention only George Brett or me when they talk about those great Royals teams of the 1970s and 1980s. But we had an All-Star team out there every night. With the exception of someplace like New York, the teams we had couldn't be assembled today because of the salaries. The guys simply were incredible.

We had Gold Glove outfielders with Otis, Willie Wilson, and Al Cowens. Mayberry had the softest hands of any first baseman in the league, and he could hit for power. Freddie Patek and U.L. Washington at shortstop were as consistent as shortstops come. And who could forget my predecessor at second, Cookie Rojas? He and Freddie made a great double-play combination at the middle infield spot for a number of years. Darrell Porter was a strong, aggressive catcher. Then there was Hal McRae, who was a great hitter and one of the most aggressive players ever. And all of those guys were just in the mid-to-late 1970s!

Our championship Royals teams, which you'll read more about throughout this book, were built through our farm system and some great trades. In fact, Jerry Terrell was the only free agent we signed in the first few years of free agency. The scouting department and general managers—men such as Cedric Tallis, Syd Thrift, and John Schuerholz—did a wonderful job of identifying and signing quality players who would help our club.

The beauty of the Royals franchise is that even from their first year as an expansion club, they didn't finish in last place until 1995. The general attitude today is that if you don't finish first, who cares. Well, the 1969 team and the early 1970s teams had pride in not finishing last. Our pride increased throughout the rest of the 1970s and 1980s when we started contending and then winning championships.

Some of that pride was lost over the last decade, culminating with the lowest point in my career in 2002, when the team lost 100 games for the first time. But my hope is that we'll regain that pride. With leaders such as

David and Dan Glass, Allard Baird, and Muzzy Jackson, we should be well on our way.

I certainly look forward to seeing what happens with our hometown Royals.

Even though Frank White was known widely for his defensive play, he became a very good clutch hitter. He was a tough out for opponents.
Photo courtesy of Kansas Collection, University of Kansas Libraries

Acknowledgments

As with most books, there seems to be too many people to thank with this one. However, if we didn't thank anyone, this would be a blank page. So to give you your money's worth by filling this page, the authors would like to thank the following personally for their hard work, dedication and support during this project.

To Doug Hoepker, Scott Cimarusti, Bob Snodgrass and the rest of the gang at Sports Publishing for their patience, guidance and desire to make this book the best book possible. To *The Kansas City Star*'s Chris Carter, who is a walking memory book.

To the Kansas City Royals organization, particularly Dave Witty for his support; to Aaron Babcock, Lora Grosshans and Chris Stathos for helping secure many of the photos, giving us unlimited access to the public relations "vault," and for research assistance. You guys are some of the best in the business. To John Martin for allowing us to reproduce your Hall of Fame paintings.

To each of the former Royals players and executives who were willing to be interviewed for this project from the outset: Dick Balderson, Buddy Blattner, Mark Gubicza, Chris Rice, John Schuerholz, John Wathan and Dave Wickersham. Special thanks to Amos Otis, Herk Robinson and Fred White, who always were accessible for some great stories and encouragement.

To Julia Akhlaghi and Rick and Amy Allen for transcribing the hours of interviews of two guys just rambling about the Royals. Your support and friendship are appreciated more than you'll know.

To Frank White for your willingness to write a great foreword. Kansas City is lucky to have you.

We each would like to thank our parents, brothers and extended families for their encouragement throughout our lives. Finally, Matt would like thank his wife, Libby, and children, Helen, Charlie, and Aaron, for their support and humoring his Elvis habits as we approached deadline. Thank you all.

Introduction

Timing is everything. Including in baseball. Ask Frank White about the keys to turning a double play, and he will stress the importance of timing on the exchange. Ask Amos Otis about stealing bases without having to slide, and he will stress the importance of timing the pitcher.

Timing meant much more for baseball in Kansas City, though. After a 13-year, love-hate relationship with Kansas City (most of which was more toward the love side until Charles O. Finley entered the picture), the Athletics moved to Oakland in October 1967. There was no baseball in Kansas City, a city that had enjoyed professional baseball since the late 1800s.

But as Major League Baseball announced expansion for 1969, Kansas City businessman Ewing Kauffman, who wasn't a big baseball fan, was urged to purchase one of the new clubs. He acquiesced. Perfect timing.

In the fall of 1968, a green, 25-year-old broadcaster named Dennis Matthews heard that baseball was expanding to Kansas City, less than eight hours from his home in Bloomington, Illinois. Matthews assembled a resume package that included photos, a demo tape, and his resume, attached it to the top of a metal Schlitz Beer serving tray (Schlitz was the title sponsor of the radio broadcasts), and sent it with a glimmer of hope.

After a successful meeting with the Royals' main announcer, Buddy Blattner, Matthews was hired. He's been with the Royals ever since. In fact, he is one of a few people who has been with the organization since day one. Perfect timing.

Within a few years after playing their first game in April 1969, the Royals became one of the most successful expansion franchises in baseball. Indeed, in 1985, after facing elimination in both the American League playoffs and the World Series, the Royals became the first expansion franchise in baseball history to win the championship. Perfect timing.

Timing also played an important role in this book. Bob Snodgrass, an acquisitions editor at Sports Publishing, started discussing this book idea with me prior to the 2003 season. Two other book projects mixed in with some procrastination delayed most of this book's writing until toward the end of the 2003 season. And, oh, what a season it was for the Royals! Perfect timing for a book.

Late in the season, Dave Witty, the Royals' vice president of broadcasting and public relations, told me about a book idea that he and

Matthews had discussed. Ironically, their idea was identical to the book I was just starting to write.

Denny and I, along with longtime announcer Fred White, worked together in 1998 on another book, *Play by Play*. So, after a brief meeting in October 2003, it made sense for Denny and me to collaborate on this book. Once again, you guessed it, perfect timing.

Reading *Tales from the Royals Dugout* is like sitting at a sports bar with Denny Matthews, surrounded by Royals memorabilia, and just listening to stories. (You don't really need the memorabilia, though, because Denny's memory and his ability to spin a tale make these stories come to life.)

Mixed in with Matthews's stories are the memories of several former players, broadcasters and front office personnel. Many of those interviews—Dick Balderson, Buddy Blattner, Mark Gubicza, Amos Otis, Herk Robinson, John Schuerholz, John Wathan, Frank White, Fred White, and Dave Wickersham—were conducted specifically for this book.

The others are from interviews I had done previously for other books or newspaper articles, including some for a feature called "Where are they now?" that currently runs in *The Kansas City Star*, and others for the Royals *Gameday* magazine.

Many of Denny's stories that follow have never been told. For the most part, a radio broadcast doesn't lend itself to the type of stories that you're about to read.

That's not to say that you're going to dig up dirt on some former Royals player. This is a book for Royals fans and anyone who enjoys good, fun baseball stories. If you had hoped to discover some trash on the Royals, put down this book and walk away.

Also, if you are hoping to find out if Amos Otis was leading the club in home runs on August 16, 1977, or what George Brett's average was on July 30, 1980, or if the Royals were in first place on May 14, 1994 (during the strike-shortened season), put down this book and walk away.

This is not a statistics-driven book or a history of the club. This book, by and large, is about the people who have made this organization one of the most successful expansion franchises in the history of baseball.

If, however, you are hoping to read some great stories—often hilarious, sometimes poignant—about this proud organization, told by someone who has lived the experiences from day one, and whose name is synonymous with the Kansas City Royals, then keep reading.

M.W.F.
December 2005

Chapter
1
IN THE BEGINNING

In 1968, after years of losing baseball and being a victim of Charlie Finley's "ingenuity" and desire to leave the Midwest, the Kansas City A's moved to Oakland. There was no longer any major league baseball in Kansas City.

Ewing Kauffman may have been one of the least obvious people to bring baseball back to Kansas City. He had developed a name for himself in pharmaceuticals and had become a billionaire through hard work. He was just a casual baseball fan, but he had the wherewithal to buy the expansion team.

I think it's safe to say that once he was pushed a little bit, he realized that he should buy the team for the city.

There were many businessmen, most of them friends of Ewing's in Kansas City, many of whom were very involved with the A's, who prodded Ewing to buy the team. Guys like Earl Smith, Les Milgram, Ernie Mehl, Charles Hughes and Charlie Truitt really got the thing rolling. And then Ewing's wife, Muriel, put him over the edge. Muriel was the last one to kick him in the seat of the pants and say, "Let's do it." Major League Baseball awarded them, and the city, the team.

Draft Day, 1968

One of the most exciting times for the franchise in the early days was drafting the team, or at least potential players for the team. I was not here yet, but my future broadcasting mentor, Buddy Blattner, who had played in the major leagues before going into broadcasting, was here and was in "the" room on draft day.

"*Cedric Tallis, the general manager, farm director Lou Gorman, and Joe Gordon, the manager, were involved in the draft, and they allowed me to sit in as well. So much homework went into it, and it was done in a systematic way. The Royals drafted according to the best available talent, not by position, and Seattle, the other expansion team, drafted by position. Seattle was hurt by that system, and the Royals came out in fine fashion with their way, actually becoming a team that was competitive right from the very go. The Royals did not say, 'We now have a second baseman, so now we need a shortstop.' They went after the best available. Then where they had ample supply, Cedric was able to trade and get a position player. It was thrilling to be a part of that draft.*"

—*Buddy Blattner*

This Is an Expansion Team?

Opening day, 1969, is one game I will remember always. The Royals, led by manager Joe Gordon, faced the Minnesota Twins, a team managed by a young and fiery Billy Martin, who was making his managerial debut. Gordon was a veteran baseball man who, ironically, had managed the Kansas City Athletics in 1960 for half of the season, in that same Municipal Stadium.

Gordon was excited about the opportunity to manage the first-year Royals. He had his first lineup almost complete after the final exhibition game in Kansas City against the St. Louis Cardinals. Ed Kirkpatrick and rookie Lou Piniella had been hitting the ball well, so they started in left field and center field, respectively, while Bob Oliver started in right. Around the infield were Chuck Harrison, Jerry Adair, Jack Hernandez and Joe Foy. Ellie Rodriguez was behind the plate. Not a bad opening-day lineup for an expansion team.

Wally Bunker

Wally Bunker was the starting pitcher on opening day in 1969. He threw the first pitch to Ted Uhlaender of the Minnesota Twins. Wally had some good years with the Baltimore Orioles before the Royals drafted him in the expansion draft. He gave us three solid years. Wally was a very quiet, soft-spoken guy, but fun to be around.

This was the group that brought major league baseball back to Kansas City in 1969. An enlarged version of this picture hangs in Stroud's Restaurant in Kansas City. I have had a standing deal with anybody who can name every person in this picture while I'm at Stroud's: their meal was on me. I have never had to buy anyone's meal.

Photo courtesy of the Kansas City Royals

Time Out for Trivia

Most people assume that the Royals' first series with the Twins was their first in front of the home crowd at Municipal Stadium. That's true if you add the first regular-season series. The Royals actually played two games prior to the opener with the Twins. The St. Louis Cardinals came into Kansas City and played exhibition games on Saturday and Sunday, before opening day.

God Must Be a Royal

Opening day, 1969, truly was amazing. Municipal Stadium probably hadn't looked that good since its debut in the 1920s. On opening day in 1969, besides the bunting that was draped over the wall along the first and third base sides, flags representing each of the major leagues' teams hung from the roof. It appeared as though baseball belonged in Kansas City. And it belonged to the Royals.

As longtime *Kansas City Star* sports editor Joe McGuff wrote in his "Sporting Comment" column on April 9, the day after the opener, "A gusty wind blew out of the south, popping the pennants that ring the roof of the stadium. One of the pennants had been partly blown down and hung in a position approaching half-mast. By the strangest sort of coincidence it was a green and gold pennant bearing the name 'Athletics.'"

A Prophetic Beginning?
Nope, Just Don Denkinger

One of the umpires for that opening day game was a guy by the name of Don Denkinger. Don Denkinger...why does that name sound so familiar? A foreshadowing? Does the sixth game of the 1985 World Series and something about a possible blown call at first base jar any mental cobwebs? Prophetic beginnings for the franchise?

Time Out for Trivia Part 2

There were three players who played for both the Kansas City A's and the Royals. Can you name them? (Hint: All three were pitchers.)

Moe Drabowsky, Dave Wickersham and Aurelio Monteagudo each played at the major-league level for both clubs.

You'll Always Remember Your First One

People often ask me about my most memorable game with the Royals. Without a doubt, it was the first one. I have more images of that game in my head than any other game that I've broadcast since opening day, Tuesday, April 8, 1969. Against the Minnesota Twins, managed by Billy Martin. How could I not say that game was my most memorable? It was my first big-league game. And, simply because of some luck, I was the first broadcaster to say "Royals win!" I owe that largely to Joe Keough.

Keough was the club's leading hitter in spring training that year with a .350 average. In the 12th inning, nearly three and a half hours after the first pitch, Keough came to the plate and ripped the first pitch from Minnesota's Dick Woodson over the head of Tony Oliva in right field. I still can picture that ball sailing over Oliva's head. There was no way he was going to get to it. The Royals won, 4-3.

"Coming out of spring training, I had planned on playing every day. As cocky as you are at that age, you're confident you can set the world on fire. Instead, I started on the bench. ... I was a little irritated that I didn't start that day. [By the time I got up,] it was so cold, I just hit the first pitch as hard as I could. ... That definitely made my highlight reel."

—Joe Keough

Dave Wickersham, who still lives in the Kansas City area, pitched five scoreless innings in relief. Moe Drabowsky got the win for Kansas City. Lou Piniella, the Royals' starting center fielder that day, was four for five as the leadoff hitter. Municipal had a crowd of 17,683 for that first game, which started at 2:32 and ended at 5:50.

"Outside of my first year in the majors, my greatest thrill was making the Royals team. It was a fresh attitude. I'm so thankful that I got to make that team. As it turned out, I pitched in the Royals' first intrasquad game, first exhibition game and on opening day. I wanted to win that one so badly. They pinch hit for me in the bottom of the 10th, Moe pitched the 11th and we won in the bottom of the 11th. Moe and I played together for a number of years, so for him to get the first win was fine. I was just happy to be there."

—Dave Wickersham

Joe Keough had a good offensive year for us in 1969, but the next season, I believe, he broke his ankle sliding into home plate and never really was quite the same. But for that one day in April of 1969, he helped give me and new Royals fans everywhere a reason to cheer...and say for the first time, "Royals win!"

As If a Dozen Wasn't Enough

What could possibly top a 12-inning thrilling win for the new home team? A 17-inning affair the next night. Bill Butler started that game for the Royals. Butler was a left-handed pitcher with good

Part of the Royals' 1969 pitching staff at the old ballpark. (From left) Tom Burgmeier, Dave Wickersham, Dick Drago and Mike Hedlund. *Photo courtesy of the Kansas City Royals*

potential. However, he never got over the hump. He had good stuff, but control problems kept his potential from materializing.

The game remained tied for the second longest in Royals history (the Royals have been involved in two 18-inning games in their history). The Royals eventually won 4-3.

Give and Take

The first loss in the club's history, in 1969, came at the hands of the Oakland A's, 5-0. Try this on for size, though. Mike Fiore, who wasn't a power hitter by any stretch, hit the first home run in Royals history—against the Oakland A's.

Dick Drago

Dick Drago pitched the Royals' first complete game. It also happened to be Drago's first major-league start. It came during a 3-2 win in Anaheim on May 2, 1969, in the nightcap of a doubleheader. The win also gave the club its first doubleheader sweep.

Building Strength up the Middle

Ask any longtime baseball person a key to winning, and sooner than later you'll hear about how it's important to build strength up the middle. That is, you want a solid catcher, second baseman, shortstop, center fielder and, of course, pitcher.

Within the span of one year, Cedric Tallis made three deals with National League teams that built the strength up the middle for Kansas City and helped solidify the team's future.

On December 3, 1969, Tallis traded Joe Foy to the Mets for Bob Johnson, a pitcher, and Amos Otis, a center fielder. Bob had a great year in 1970, and it was obvious after Amos's first year with the Royals that he was going to be a star.

Then in the middle of the 1970 season, Cookie Rojas came to the Royals from the Cardinals for an outfielder named Fred Rico (no, he never did anything in the big leagues).

Almost a year to the day after the initial deal with the Mets, on December 2, 1970, Cedric took Johnson, who had had a good season—could throw hard and was goofy as hell—and sent him to the Pirates for Jerry May, a catcher, Bruce Dal Canton, a pitcher, and Fred Patek, a shortstop.

So in those three deals, Cedric got a catcher, a pitcher, a second baseman, a shortstop, and a center fielder. Boom, strength up the middle right away. That was a building block for many years.

The Royals Baseball Academy

Ewing Kauffman was an innovator and a smart businessman. With those qualities in mind, Ewing wanted to find a way to improve on his investment.

One of the unique plans that Ewing devised to develop the franchise was the Royals Baseball Academy. Basically, his thought was to

The Royals' first general manager, Cedric Tallis (left) and manager Joe Gordon at the old ballpark. *Photo courtesy of the Kansas City Royals*

take players who had not been drafted—and who were good athletes—train them through intense work, and mold them into Royals baseball players.

He felt that the organization could take great athletes and turn them into productive major leaguers. So in August 1970, he started the Royals Baseball Academy in Sarasota, Florida, with longtime baseball man Syd Thrift as the academy's director.

"The academy was just starting to blossom during my fourth year in the minor leagues. Syd, who had signed me, brought a few of us minor league guys down to the academy to participate and enhance some of the academy players. During three winters I pitched and got my feet wet with the

academy. As time went on, they began drafting players and putting them in the academy. I think people laughed at Mr. Kauffman and the organization for this kind of experiment. I think it has some merit. I still think to this day, if you went back to basics, you could get some great players. But it was a very costly venture back then. It definitely had an outstanding facility. I think Baltimore still uses it as a minor league facility."

—Dick Balderson, who, after spending a few seasons in the Royals' minor leagues as a player, became John Schuerholz's assistant. Dick now works with Schuerholz and the Atlanta Braves.

Forming the academy was an example of the way Mr. K's mind worked. He was very competitive, always looking for something different, looking for an edge. Some of the other baseball minds in the organization thought that the Baseball Academy had some merit and decided to give it a shot. Even if people didn't like the idea, they went with it because it was something that Mr. K wanted to try.

"Ewing invited me and my wife to spend some time with him on his yacht to pick my brain about the academy. We talked about the negative and positive factors. I said, 'I know you have the financial means to do this, and you are going to get 90 percent of the people who say it can't be done. You want it to happen; why don't you do it? You might be unhappy the rest of your life if you don't do it. If you can afford the failure, for goodness sakes, do it.' Several people around the organization told him to try it, and he did. Things just didn't work out."

—Buddy Blattner

The academy was designed as a two-year program (including college), so a high school diploma was a must for a hopeful. During the morning, at Ewing's insistence, each player was expected to attend school at Manatee Junior College. He insisted that they take some speaking courses and some personal finance courses. He wanted them to be able to mingle in society, to talk to the press and to be able to handle their money. So the players went to college in the mornings and studied baseball for the remainder of the day.

Coaches at the Royals Baseball Academy in 1970 (from left) Frank Evans, Syd Thrift, trainer Harry Ledford and Steve Korcheck. Notice the names on the blackboard—Frank White at third base? *Photo courtesy of the Kansas City Royals*

In April 1974, the Royals Baseball Academy closed. But as it turned out, it was too bad that the experiment ended. The Royals got their middle infield of the late 1970s and into the 80s out of the academy: Frank White (the academy's first and best "graduate") and U.L. Washington.

Bob Taylor

Bob "Hawk" Taylor hit a pinch-hit home run in Detroit during our first year that I always will remember. The Tigers, in 1969, were a very good team. The Royals, obviously, were just trying to be competitive. Hawk Taylor, who grew up in Metropolis, Illinois, could catch, play the outfield and even play a little first base. But he was a terrific pinch hitter.

Heading into the top of the ninth inning, on May 6, 1969, Detroit's Denny McLain was cruising with a 6-2 lead. The Royals put a rally together and chased McLain out of the game. Finally, with two on and two out, Hawk Taylor went to the plate to pinch hit for the Royals with the Tigers leading 6-4. Dick Radatz was now pitching for Detroit.

Hawk got hold of a pitch and drove it onto the roof in left center, approximately 440 feet. It was a blast. The Royals held on for a 7-6 win. That win put the Royals at 14-11 on the season.

After Hawk hit the homer, Ewing and Muriel Kauffman, who hardly ever were seen at a Royals road game, were on the roof of the dugout, dancing and cheering. Mr. K was not flamboyant, so to see that enthusiasm in an amazing emotional win was special.

On the Road Again

Early in my career, it was thrilling to travel around the country with a major league team. It was great to see the sights and the different ballparks. Road trips in those early years also produced some hilarious memories for me.

For instance, when the team went to Minneapolis, it stayed in the Leamington Hotel, which was one of the worst places we stayed in those early years. It wasn't a well-run place. There would be a basket of fruit in your room, but the fruit would be two weeks old.

We arrived there late on a Sunday night from somewhere, and everyone was extremely tired. Guys just wanted to get to their rooms and crash. The bags came off the luggage truck and into the lobby, where there was only one bellman on duty. This guy had to be in his mid-80s, with two or three teeth. He was getting the bags together but moved at the speed of a glacier.

One of the players asked, "How long before I get my bags to my room?"

Another one shouted a reply: "Wednesday!"

Hey Kids, Big Ben, Parliament...

When we played in Washington, D.C. against the Senators, we stayed at the Shoreham Hotel, which was about a 30-minute ride from the ballpark. I always have a hard time with direction in D.C. because everything is in a circle around a hub. I guess I'm not the only one with trouble.

We played on a Saturday afternoon, and after the game we were on the bus headed back to the hotel. We pulled up to an intersection, and I noticed a barbershop named Shorty's on the corner. About 10 minutes later, we pulled up to an intersection, and there was another barbershop named Shorty's. It looked similar to the first, but no big deal. Then it happened a third time. Radio producer-engineer Ed Shepherd said, "Man, this Shorty must be doing pretty well, because he has a chain of barbershops all over town."

Actually, no, he didn't. We had been going in circles. The bus driver was lost.

The Moonlighting Bus Driver

We arrived at Chicago's Midway Airport real late one night after playing in Texas. We had lost two out of three to the Rangers. So nobody was in a good mood, plus everyone was tired. Midway to downtown was about a 20-minute drive.

The bus driver, who was black, fancied himself as an entertainer. He got on the bus microphone and said something about how it was a nice night out, and then he told a joke. A bad joke. The groans gave that away.

Evidently, the bus driver felt that one went so well that he launched into another joke. It wasn't very good, either. Now the guys were getting restless and basically telling the guy to stop and just drive. John Mayberry, from his seat in the back, said, "C'mon, get off the brother. Let him do his thing!"

The driver told another bad joke. Somebody from the middle of the bus fired another insult. Big John again said, "C'mon, get off the brother." This cycle went on a few more times. It wasn't getting any better.

The driver told one more bad joke. Finally Big John shouted, "OK, guys ... get on the brother!"

The whole bus just broke up.

Chapter
2
THE
CHAMPIONSHIP YEARS

Although the Royals had a rough first few seasons, the organization has enjoyed a success not shared by many other expansion clubs. In fact, as early as the team's third season, it had a winning record and finished in second place in the American League West.

In 1975, despite winning 91 games—which is still a tie for the fourth most wins in club history—the Royals still finished second in the division.

Then, in 1976, the Royals broke through. They won 90 games, but more importantly, they won their first American League West division championship. Kansas City went on to win the division three of the next four years. In all, the Royals have won their division six times (1976-78, 1980, 1984 and 1985).

In addition, they finally overcame the rival New York Yankees in the 1980 ALCS and earned a spot in the World Series, where they lost to Philadelphia, four games to two.

Finally! In 1985, the club won its first World Series championship, defeating cross-state rival St. Louis four games to three, after a seven-game series win against Toronto in the ALCS. By winning that Series, the Royals became the first American League expansion club, and second expansion club in major-league history, to win the world championship.

The following are some of Matthews's most vivid memories from those championship seasons.

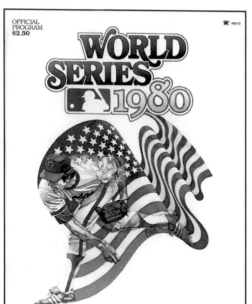

Two magical seasons for the Royals.

Program covers courtesy of the Kansas City Royals

1985

Since the 1985 World Series victory was the culmination of 17 seasons of hard work, rough times, heartbreaking losses, and fantastic people, it seems like a logical place to start this chapter.

The Dominator

When people ask me if there is a game or a moment from George Brett's career that sticks out to me, without hesitation I point to the third game of the 1985 American League Championship Series against Toronto.

With the Royals trailing two games to none and playing the first of three in Kansas City, Brett basically willed himself to lead the team to a win. If the Royals lost that game, they would have been done in the series, because they probably would not have won four straight.

But Brett wasn't going to let that happen. Offensively and defensively, he controlled the game for Kansas City. A pitcher can dominate or control a game. It's hard for a position player to dominate a game, though, because he is only going to bat four or five times. Defensively he can't dominate unless a high number of balls are hit his way. So there isn't much that a position player can do. However, Brett did.

The stars were aligned properly for that, and George responded. He made huge plays at third, he homered twice, and doubled twice. The Royals won 6-5.

To me, that was George's best, biggest and most important moment at that time in Royals history.

Down Three to One? Hey, No Sweat

The Royals were not favored in either postseason series in 1985. Toronto had home-field advantage in the American League playoffs, and the Cardinals were supposedly the best team in baseball. Still, the Royals felt some normal pressure early in each series. Until they got down ... big. When the Royals went down three games to one in each of those series, the pressure was off. They used the fact they were not favored and down three to one to their advantage. It allowed them to relax.

The Tarp That Helped Kansas City

Vince Coleman was one of the fastest players in the game while he was playing. But in a bizarre accident before the World Series, Coleman, who was a rookie in 1985 for the Cardinals, couldn't outrun the tarp! The tarp in St. Louis rolled over Coleman's leg, and he was out for the series.

Coleman was at the top of the St. Louis lineup, and everybody fit in nicely behind him. Once he went down, their whole batting order changed. In turn, St. Louis didn't hit a lick in the series.

Terry Pendleton, who was with the Cardinals in 1985 and spent his last big-league season with the Royals in 1998, told me that when Coleman went out, they were a completely different team.

And May the Best Team Win ... Or Something Like That

Statistically, St. Louis was the best team in baseball that season. They won 102 games and were the only team to win more than 100 games that year. However, the World Series came down to seven games, and the Royals were the best team for that stretch.

The week after the World Series ended, I was on a radio talk show in St. Louis, and I knew what was coming. Sure enough, the second caller said, "Can you honestly sit there in Kansas City and see all the Royals games and tell me that you think the Royals are better than the Cardinals?"

I replied: "Let me put it to you this way. The Cardinals were the best team in baseball this year—for six months. Over 162 games, they won 102. Nobody else won 100, so the Cardinals were the best team in baseball in 1985. However, in seven games in October, the Royals out-hit the Cardinals, outpitched the Cardinals, outdefended the Cardinals, outplayed the Cardinals and played with more poise. So the Royals, for those seven games, were better than the Cardinals. Would you agree with both statements?"

After a long pause the guy finally said, "Well, since you put it that way, I can see your point."

Enough said.

"It's impossible for me to pick a favorite World Series championship. However, 1985 was the first world championship I was involved with. The first one was very special. I will never forget the feeling I had in the clubhouse after we won. It was tremendous. We might not have had the best talent in 1985, but we were the best team in 1985."

—John Schuerholz, who, as general manager, has guided the Royals and Atlanta Braves to World Series wins

The Call

Of course, all non-Royals fans want to point to umpire Don Denkinger's call at first base, ruling Jorge Orta was safe, when the replay showed that he was probably out. Enough has been said and written about the call that I'm not going to rehash it here. But it's interesting to me how each side has its own take on that play from the sixth game of the Series.

"That World Series was great for the state of Missouri. It was a World Series where we didn't score any runs. The Royals pitching staff was outstanding. We only scored 14 runs in seven games. We should have won the World Series in six games, though, because we were leading 1-0 when we had that famous call at first. We self-destructed after that. If [Orta] had been called out at first—everybody knew he was out—the Series would have been over."

—Whitey Herzog

"But we scored the winning run with one out. We still had an out to play if the play went differently at first. The way things had been going for us that season, who's to say that whoever was coming up next doesn't hit a home run and we win anyhow. It was a magical season for us. [The Cardinals] had every opportunity in the world to come back in Game 7, but we blew them away. Darryl Motley set the tone in that game when he hit the ball foul and then hit it out. Hey, they had us down three games to one. If you can't close it out at three games to one, don't blame it on the umpire.

Yeah, [the call] went our way, but still they were up three games to one. You have to be able to close out a team when you have them down like that."

—*Mark Gubicza*

Bring Out the Hit-O-Meter

There seems to always be an unsung hero in the World Series. And it seems it's normally an unsuspecting infielder. Buddy Biancalana filled that role and reached his claim to fame during the 1985 World Series. Thanks to a fantasy series for him at shortstop, and talk show host David Letterman, Buddy became a household name for several weeks in October that year.

I remember Buddy, who was a first-round draft pick, working out for the Royals for the first time after he signed. We were in Oakland. It was obvious that he needed to get stronger, but defensively he had really good hands and good actions. He had all the tools to be a good defensive player.

During the 1985 World Series, Buddy Biancalana became a household name. *Photo courtesy of the Kansas City Royals*

Buddy ended up being a solid shortstop and an important part of that world championship. He had a terrific postseason.

"The World Series was a fabulous experience for me, as people can imagine, but taking it to a different level, that was the best baseball I had ever played. I reached a level of concentration that I never experienced prior to that time. I don't know how I got there except that for the first time I acknowledged fear—the fear that I experienced prior to Game 1 of the World Series.

"I'll never forget sitting on my chair in front of my locker prior to the [first] game, about a half-hour before ABC wanted us on the foul line. I started thinking, 'Oh my, this is really intense.' I figured I could put on my street clothes and go watch the game on TV somewhere, or I could grab my glove, walk down the runway and take the field. Obviously I'm glad I made the choice that I made."

—*Buddy Biancalana*

If memory serves me correctly, Letterman had what he called the "Hit-O-Meter" late in the 1985 season. He used it to compare Pete Rose and Buddy in "their" chase for Ty Cobb's all-time hits record. At the time, Rose had more than 4,000 major-league hits, and Buddy was around 50 major-league hits. Buddy, who was very outgoing, made a couple appearances on Letterman's show and did very well, just as he did in the World Series.

The Pitching Staff

One of the biggest reasons the 1985 team was so successful was its young pitching staff. They came together at the same time with the mentality that the starters were going to go as long as they could, and then the relievers would come in and finish off the opponent. Each of those guys had a great attitude.

"We had so many young guys coming up at the same time that we were feeding off everyone. Plus, we got a lot of experience in 1984, and getting to the playoffs against a great Tigers team was huge. There was Danny Jackson, Bret Saberhagen, Charlie Leibrandt, who was older than us, but he didn't

have a lot of experience, Bud Black, who was the senior of the staff but he was still relatively young in baseball terms, and me. We were all fairly talented and we had fun together. At that point, we really didn't know the magnitude of what was going to happen in terms of the playoffs and World Series, so everyone just had a good time feeding off each other. We also were helped when Dick Howser came in and said that he had five number-one guys instead of one number-one guy. That gave us confidence to go out there when it was our turn and perform."

—Mark Gubicza

That staff was a good mix of young guys, veterans, lefties and righties. Throughout the entire season, the bigger the game, the better they pitched. That was the element they brought. Lesser guys wouldn't have pitched as well. Our guys accepted the challenge.

"Our pitching staff in 1985 was outstanding. They certainly were talented enough to be world champions. We couldn't have asked them to do more than they did. We built that team around pitching, defense, and speed, and it paid off."

—John Schuerholz

During the World Series, Kansas City's pitching staff held St. Louis to only 13 runs and a .185 batting average. According to the Royals' media guide, that was the lowest-ever batting average in a seven-game World Series.

Charlie Cool

Charlie Leibrandt, a lefty who came to the Royals in a trade in June 1983, added the element of finesse and experience to the young pitching staff that eventually won the 1985 World Series. Charlie was in Kansas City until 1989, and I think it's safe to say that his best years were with the Royals.

Although Charlie easily was not the hardest thrower on that 1985 staff, he had good stuff and was one of the most competitive guys on the club. Bret Saberhagen, Danny Jackson, Mark Gubicza—all those guys—

threw harder than Charlie Leibrandt. But Charlie broke more opponents' bats than probably all of those other pitchers combined because he had that great knack of pitching inside. He was great at getting in on a hitter's hands.

He was perfect for that pitching staff because he was the "old hand," the experienced guy, and he took some pressure off the younger guys. In turn, those other guys were so good that they took pressure off Charlie. It was a perfect blend of experience and youth.

The Man in the Clutch

Danny Jackson pitched and won, in my opinion, two of the most significant games in Royals history. Both were in 1985. Both were in the postseason. Both were Game 5.

In 1985, the American League Championship Series had gone from a best-of-five series to a best-of-seven series. As fate would have it, the Royals were down three games to one against Toronto, facing elimination. Jackson came out and shut out the Blue Jays in the fifth game.

Wouldn't you know it, the Royals faced a similar situation in the World Series. Kansas City was down three games to one. Jackson went to the mound in St. Louis and held the Cardinals to one run on five hits. In the game, he retired St. Louis batters in order five times.

In both the ALCS and the World Series, with his team facing elimination, Jackson went out and got the job done.

Tending to His Flock

Catcher Jim Sundberg was one of the spark plugs of the 1985 championship team. He was as important as anyone on that club. He was very durable despite his size, because he wasn't built like a catcher. But he contributed a great deal, especially working with that young pitching staff. Sunny brought needed stability to that staff.

When Sunny was young, he was as quick and as flexible as anybody I had ever seen behind the plate. He was almost like a goalie in hockey. But even more than that, as a veteran in Kansas City, he gave the club a mature, experienced guy behind home plate. He was perfect for that team and that pitching staff.

Away from the field, Sunny is a gem of a guy, which made it even easier to root for him.

Skates

Everywhere Lonnie Smith went, his team won. Kansas City was no exception. The Royals traded with the Cardinals in May 1985 to obtain Smith. Kansas City traded John Morris, a player who never appeared on the big-league field for the Royals.

Lonnie was nicknamed "Skates" because of his misadventures in the outfield. He had the reputation of being a terrible defensive player. For the most part, that's probably true. Somebody once said that the only reason Lonnie Smith wore a glove was because it was a league tradition. However, Lonnie was a great offensive player and a terrific base runner.

The Royals were in Milwaukee when Lonnie joined the club. That night he was in left field. A ball was hit into the corner at County Stadium, and Skates hit the wall as hard as any Royals player I had seen. BAM! You could hear that all over the ballpark. He staggered backwards after the vicious collision. That was just the way he played. Whitey Herzog loved Lonnie in St. Louis because he was a tough, hard-nosed player.

But it's amazing to look at Lonnie's career and see how championships have followed him. Sure, coincidence is involved, but he was a great leadoff guy. He found a way to get on base and found a way to get around the bases.

Lonnie was fun to watch in the outfield. He started to make a throw from left field one night, and the ball slipped out of his hand. And he just spiked it. The ball ended up three feet in front of him and almost buried in the grass. It was actually pretty funny.

Skates deserves credit, though. Every time he was with a team that was in range of a championship, it won, and it was in no small part because of him and his ability to score runs. He was a championship just waiting to happen.

Second Time's a Charm

Darryl Motley was one of those players who everybody thought would have a great impact on this organization. Even though he wasn't a career impact player, he certainly left his mark on the club in 1985.

In the second inning of the seventh game, Motley hit a home run that really gave the Royals momentum. Early in that at-bat, he drilled one down the left field line that went foul by a few feet. Then he crushed a pitch and got back those few extra feet. Two-run home run.

Motley also made the final catch, sealing the Royals' 11-0 win and first World Series championship.

"Right before the inning, Willie [Wilson] and I were jogging onto the field. We played catch before the inning, and Willie mentioned how he was going to catch the last out [of the game]. I told him I was going to beat him to the ball. [With two outs, Andy] Van Slyke hit it toward right center. I got there first, but I could hear Willie coming. I think I would've been more nervous if we were only up by one run when that ball was coming down. But I caught it and I still have it."

—Darryl Motley

The Royals at the White House, October 31, 1985. Manager Dick Howser is about to present a Royals jacket to President Ronald Reagan. Muriel Kauffman looks on approvingly. *Photo courtesy of Denny Matthews*

The Royals' Father Figure

Ewing Kauffman realized that playing in the World Series was the culmination of what the team had been trying to do. So, like a father figure in his quiet way, he was proud when the Royals went in 1980, and he was especially proud when they went again in 1985. He never did get really close to the players; he was seldom in the clubhouse and he didn't socialize with them, but he was a "proud father." It was almost as if he was saying, "Here's my boy, finally becoming a man and establishing himself as a champion."

I don't recall even seeing Ewing much in 1985. He didn't come to the clubhouse much after the games or go to the parade after the team won the Series. He didn't do any of that. He was pleased for all the people who had been working toward that end, and he was happy for the fans who came to the ballpark and supported the team. He was very happy to see them rewarded for supporting the team. That was his mindset all the time. He could see that they were being rewarded, so he was being rewarded.

1984

Home (Run), James

Jamie Quirk has meant a great deal to this organization. But James's biggest contribution to the Royals was a home run he hit for the Indians to beat the Twins. That homer clinched the 1984 Western Division title for the Royals. People want to talk about Babe Ruth's called shot ... Jamie's might be better.

The Royals battled the Twins much of the 1984 season in the AL West. Late in that season, Jamie was being traded to the Indians (not from the Royals, mind you). Before going to Cleveland, he stopped in Kansas City and went to Paul Splittorff's retirement party. As Jamie was getting ready to leave the party, he shouted to the partygoers, "Don't worry about it. I'll help win one for you."

A few days later, in his only at-bat in a Cleveland uniform, Jamie knocked one of the longest home runs of his career. It went into the upper deck at Cleveland's old stadium. We were getting on an airplane to travel to the West Coast when we heard about the home run. What a feeling! The Royals won earlier that day, so Jamie Quirk's homer helped put the Twins too far out of first to catch K.C.

The Royals were swept by Detroit in the playoffs, but what a called shot by Jamie Quirk!

1980

The 1980 season, which was one of the hottest summers in Kansas City history, was magical in many ways for the Royals as a franchise. That was the season of no race for us. In fact, the Royals clinched the division on September 17, which was the earliest the club has ever wrapped up the division. They finished the regular season with a 14-game lead in the standings.

The Only Race of the Year

The biggest question mark during the regular season was whether George Brett was going to finish with a .400 batting average, the highest since Ted Williams hit .406 more than 30 years earlier.

George did not have the pressure of team success in his chase for .400, because after the end of May, the Royals ran away with the division. He had several hot streaks that year. One thing I remember was that toward the end of the season, when the media blitz really started, the Royals held a daily 20-minute press conference with George. I always thought that was good, because George didn't have to be concerned with answering the same questions 72 times.

George basically hit the ball hard all season. That likely was the hardest he hit the ball, consistently, during his Hall of Fame career. If he had gotten just five or six more hits, he would have reached .400 instead of .390.

George still vividly remembers when he went over .400 against Toronto.

"They walked [John Wathan] on four pitches and loaded the bases. With each ball to him, the crowd roared louder and louder because I was on deck at .399. We were leaving town the next day, so I guess everybody wanted to see me get that next at-bat. I ended up hitting one over the left fielder's head for a bases-clearing double. The ovation was unbelievable. I looked

around and saw [the average at .401] and saw the standing ovation, so I just took my hat off and raised my arms up. Little did I know what was going to happen over the next six weeks of the season. I didn't realize how hectic it was going to be. Really, there wasn't any buildup at .390 or .395 or .397. All of a sudden, I got to .400 and for the next month that was all that I talked about.

"I enjoyed [the experience], I guess. At times the attention and the press conferences that I had to do before and after every ballgame kind of alienated me a little bit. But when the season was over and I had a chance to look at it, I realized it was fun and I hoped that I'd have another chance to do that again. I was 27 years old and coming into my prime, and thought that it might be possible again. ... Obviously I never had a chance to get that hot again.

"I've thought about how my life would be different if I had ended at .400. And, obviously, it wouldn't be any different. But to be the last guy to reach that milestone is a great moniker to have by your name. It would be unbelievable. To come so close and fail, yeah, I'm disappointed by it."

—*George Brett*

Getting Past the Yanks...Finally!

As you'll read about in the next chapter, the Royals and Yankees had a great rivalry during the 1970s, largely sparked by New York's dominance over Kansas City in the American League playoffs. In 1980, it was the Royals' turn to dominate.

With Kansas City leading the ALCS against New York two games to none, the teams headed to the Bronx with the Royals cautiously optimistic. In the top of the fifth inning of the Friday night game, the Royals took a 1-0 lead when Frank White homered.

The Yankees, however, came back with two runs in the bottom of the sixth.

In the top of the seventh, the Royals deflated the Yankees for good. With two outs in the inning, Willie Wilson and U.L. Washington were on base for the Royals. That set up a meeting between George Brett and the Yankees' dominant closer, "Goose" Gossage.

Brett launched the first-pitch fastball into the upper deck in right field. I don't think Yankee Stadium ever has been that quiet during the season. That completely put a worm in New York's apple. And it propelled the Royals to the World Series.

"That, by far, was the biggest hit of my career. Ever. Especially after losing to [the Yankees] three straight years—'76, '77 and '78.

"Time flies, but I can remember all of it so vividly. I remember rounding the bases and how quiet Yankee Stadium got. It was a great thrill not only to beat them but to get the hit that beat them. Usually when we were there it was the loudest place you'd ever been. To get a hit that silenced everybody was unbelievable."

—George Brett

"I played right field in the last inning when Dan Quisenberry struck out Willie Randolph. I remember running back toward the infield for the celebration. It was the only time in my whole career that I cried on the field. It almost felt like we were world champs already."

—John Wathan

Should We Stay or Should We Go?

Even though Fred White and I knew that the playoffs would be the last games we'd broadcast that season, we decided to stay with the team through the first part of the World Series. The only problem was that we didn't know where the Royals would be playing. The Royals-Yankees series ended on a Friday night. Philadelphia and Houston still were playing their series. And the World Series wouldn't be starting until Tuesday.

So we hung around New York for three days. The final Philadelphia-Houston game was on Sunday night in Houston. We were in the airport, in New York, with our TWA charter and about 125 people in our traveling party, instead of our usual 50 or 55 people, waiting to see what would happen in Houston.

Obviously, the Phillies won, so we took a 22-minute flight to Philadelphia. We went into Philly on Sunday night and worked out at Veterans Stadium on Monday night. And then we played on Tuesday. So we didn't play from Friday night to Tuesday night, which is a pretty long layoff, even that late in the season.

"I think [staying in New York] hurt us in the World Series. I think it was a poor decision to spend those three days in New York, while everybody was celebrating like crazy in Kansas City. Had we been able to ride that wave of enthusiasm from the city, and gone back to Kansas City, I think we would have been in better shape going into Philadelphia. But to sit around in New York for three days and wait, and not see what was going on in Kansas City, I think it was a letdown."

—*John Wathan*

The Phillies were a good team. They had pitchers Steve Carlton and Tug McGraw and a good hitting lineup. That long layoff, and the fact we finally beat the Yankees really affected the Royals in the World Series. It was almost as if beating the Yankees was the Royals' World Series.

"I really believe that our World Series was won when we beat the Yankees. Not that we were flat, but when you looked at [Houston and Philadelphia] on paper, we felt we better matched up with Houston. When the Phillies won, I think we were a little disappointed. ... But that experience whet our appetites about the World Series. The World Series wasn't beating the New York Yankees; it was beating someone from the other league. Sure enough we had that opportunity in 1985 and took advantage of it."

—*George Brett*

That was the time when Brett had the physical problem with the hemorrhoids. Willie Wilson didn't have a good series, striking out 12 times, I believe, which really hurt.

In fact, the only two players who stood out were Willie Aikens and Amos Otis. Otis hit .478 during the series with three home runs, and Aikens belted four homers.

It was a well played series, and the Royals had their chances, but they couldn't capitalize. Take nothing away from the Phillies, though.

They were a good team. Carlton won two games, including the decisive sixth game, in which he struck out seven and gave up only four hits. And McGraw, who passed away in early January 2004, had one win, one loss and two saves in the series.

1976

For many, the 1976 loss in the playoffs to the Yankees was the most difficult to swallow. Even though it was Kansas City's first foray into the postseason, the Royals were on the cusp of winning it and going to the World Series.

Heading into the series finale, Game 5, each team had won one and lost one at home. The Royals won the fourth game, in New York, 7-4.

Then, heading into the bottom of the ninth of Game 5, the teams were tied 6-6. In the bottom of the inning, Chris Chambliss lifted a homer barely over the right field fence, and game, set and match went to the Yankees. Although this might sound harsh, Amos Otis's absence from the lineup is the reason the Royals lost the 1976 AL playoffs. In his first at-bat at Royals Stadium in Game 1, A.O. hit first base wrong and turned his ankle. He missed the rest of the playoffs. That forced Whitey Herzog to move Al Cowens from right to center and put Hal McRae in right.

Mac wasn't a bad outfielder, but he was considerably shorter than Al. Whitey maintains to this day that if Cowens had been playing right field, he would have caught the ball that Chambliss eked over the fence for the homer.

Plus, the fact that we didn't have Amos for any of the five games (besides the first inning of Game 1) really hurt the Royals' chances. Of course, there are other factors, and every pitch in that series was different after Otis went down, but his turned ankle was a big factor in the Royals' loss of the 1976 playoffs. It changed the Royals' lineup both offensively and defensively—sound familiar? See Vince Coleman and St. Louis, 1985.

"I don't think 1976 was a disappointment. It was a tough loss, but no one gave us much of a chance to do much that year anyway. The 1977 team was the best team I've ever managed. Even though we won three pennants

and a World Series in St. Louis, and played some good defense, the 1977 Royals team was the best team I ever had. We had the Yankees down two games to one. That was a playoff we should have won."

—*Whitey Herzog*

That 1976 series helped kick-start the rivalry between the Royals and the Yankees.

Chapter
3
YANKEES AND A'S AND CARDS, OH MY!

The Royals have had a few great rivalries since 1969. Of course, they aren't the longstanding rivalries such as the Dodgers and Giants enjoy, or the Yankees and Red Sox. But since day one, Kansas City has had some good ones, including the A's, Yankees, White Sox, Rangers and Cardinals.

Since the beginning of the Royals' existence, they had a natural rival: the Oakland A's. Since the A's left Kansas City high and dry, fans really wanted the Royals to crush the A's. There were many hard feelings. But that really helped us build a fan base. We haven't seen that intense distaste since. By 1973-74, the Royals were becoming a contender and the A's were tremendous. It was frustrating until 1976, when the Royals finally beat the A's for the American League West championship.

But when that happened, the Yankees were waiting in the wings. New York became the main rival because the Royals and Yankees played in the playoffs four out of five years. That lasted until 1980.

Those two rivalries, the A's and Yankees, were by far the best in Royals history. Whatever has followed has paled by comparison. The excitement and atmosphere of the games with the A's and Yankees is unparalleled.

There have been some years where we had some intense games with the teams, nearing rivalry status, but none of those was anything like the A's and Yankees.

The rivalry with the White Sox lasted most of one season, until the Royals pulled away in the standings in August. The Royals and Rangers also had a mini-rivalry, but that was based more on brawls than anything else.

The only other rivalry that comes to mind is the Cardinals. That one started with the 1985 World Series and has been allowed to continue through interleague play. It's not a great rivalry, because we play them only three or six times a year, but it could be fantastic. It's kind of a shame we don't play more.

Just What Does "A" Stand For?

When Charlie Finley moved the A's to Oakland, most fans in Kansas City said good riddance. Finley's tasteless antics had left a bad ... well, taste ... in the mouths of Kansas Citians. So when the Royals came into existence in 1969, so did the rivalry with the A's.

During the heated years of the rivalry, there was electricity, cheating, brawls and a dramatic Royals win that capped everything. There was a different type of atmosphere around the ballpark when the A's came to town. There were hard feelings about them leaving, and you could sense that when they returned to play.

Vida Leaves Royals Feeling Blue

Even though fans enjoyed watching Vida Blue pitch for the Royals during 1982-83, one of my best memories of him was when he came to Kansas City with the Oakland A's for a game at Municipal Stadium. It was August 3, 1971, a Friday night, and the two teams were bitter rivals at the time.

Vida Blue was the phenom, and everybody wanted to see him pitch. It was an electric night. Unfortunately, the Royals' front office wasn't expecting quite the number of fans that showed up. They were stunned. People just kept coming and coming.

The team was expecting about 20,000 or so, and it had a record-breaking crowd of 35,623. At the time, that was the largest crowd ever to see major league baseball in Kansas City. The previous record was set earlier in the 1971 season, 35,295, to see the Angels.

Besides the rivalry, that game may have been set up largely by the pitching duel that Blue and Kenny Wright got into earlier in the season. On May 14, in Vida's first appearance in Kansas City, Wright gave up only four hits through eight innings, and the Royals had a 3-0 lead in the ninth.

During the ninth inning, in which Kenny was taken out, Oakland scored five runs and went on to win the game 5-3. That was Kansas City's introduction to Vida Blue.

And You Thought the Raiders Were the Bad Boys in Oakland

During a late September series in Oakland in 1976, tensions were high between the clubs. The Royals held an advantage in the West standings, but the A's were inching closer. Additionally, a week earlier, in Kansas City, A's pitcher Stan Bahnsen had hit Amos Otis in the head with a pitch. Otis missed several games after that.

"There was some bad blood there. I ran across a few of Oakland's pitchers at a mall the day before I got hit. They told me that they were going to hit me. The first two pitches were away from the plate; the next pitch was about a foot behind me. Seeing the ball coming toward me, I naturally leaned back. When I did that, it hit me on the side of the helmet, in the temple, and knocked me cold. I couldn't get my helmet on my head for a week with the knot that I had."

—Amos Otis

On September 28, the two teams were playing in Oakland. Dennis Leonard was on the mound for the Royals. In the first inning, Leo nailed Oakland's Don Baylor, who was among league leaders in getting hit by pitches because he crowded the plate. Baylor, who was a big bull of a man, charged the mound.

Leonard took one step in and then immediately went toward shortstop. George Brett came over from third base and tried to intercept Baylor. Baylor evidently didn't notice George because he brushed Brett aside as if he wasn't there. Baylor just wanted a piece of Leo.

By that time, the bases were cleared. The dugouts were empty. That thing went on for several minutes, with several good punches being thrown.

"Our pitchers were good at retaliating at whoever you wanted them to get. Dennis Leonard asked me who I wanted. I pointed to Don Baylor. Leo nailed him. That fight went on for what seemed like forever. I kept walking around, looking for Stan Bahnsen, but I could never find him. That night was a mess."

—Amos Otis

Later in the ballgame, there was a skirmish around the Royals' bullpen. I don't know what set off that little melee, but all of a sudden two or three fans and a couple of Royals were pushing and shoving.

Then, the fans started coming down the aisle toward the bullpen area. A fan would run down, and a Royals player would deck him. Then somebody else would come down, and he'd get knocked around. At some point during all of this, either Hal McRae or Tommy Davis grabbed an umbrella from one of the fans and hit somebody over the head with it.

Of course, the next morning's Oakland newspaper in 1976 had that bullpen fracas pictured on the front page. It sure was ugly that night, but things got much better the next day.

Ending the Seven-Year Itch

The next night, Wednesday, September 29, the Royals clinched at least a tie for their first division title, behind two stars of the game: one unlikely and one unlikely, Larry Gura and Otis. The game truly was a defining moment in the Royals' history. The Royals had finally caught the team that had been a thorn in their side for seven years. (The Royals clinched outright a few days later at home.)

Manager Whitey Herzog made a shocking move by starting pitcher Gura and catcher John Wathan in that game. Most of the guys thought Whitey was out of his mind. Didn't he realize this was a chance for the Royals to clinch their first ever pennant? Didn't he realize that one of the other starting pitchers and catcher Buck Martinez should make up the battery in this important game?

Whitey showed us why he was manager. He felt the A's lineup would have more trouble against the crafty left-hander Gura than any other pitcher in the team's rotation. He was right.

"*Larry Gura was a good finesse pitcher. When I was called up in 1976, he had come over from the Yankees. I was the third catcher that year. We were going into a big series against Oakland at the end of the season. We were losing, and not playing very well, and we were trying to catch them. Larry had been pitching a lot in the bullpen, but not starting much. Whitey decided to start him against the A's, and he asked Larry who he wanted to catch for him. He said he wanted me to. Larry ended up throwing a 4-0 shutout, and that clinched a tie for our first division championship. That was a great night for me.*"

—*John Wathan*

Amos Otis helped add some fuel to the rivalry with the A's and then came up big for the Royals in the 1976 game that separated them from the former team that occupied Kansas City. *Photo courtesy of the Kansas City Royals*

The expected star, Otis, wasn't expected to play. He had been benched for the first two games of the series. In fact, he hadn't played much over the previous two weeks after being hit in the head by Bahnsen. However, after several players lobbied Herzog, Whitey decided to put A.O. in the lineup. Another huge move by the White Rat.

Otis didn't disappoint. He shone with an RBI double and a two-run home run as the Royals won 4-0. After the game, the Royals were chanting "A.O., A.O., A.O."—a chant normally reserved for fans at Royals Stadium—as Otis boarded the team bus.

"That's a very special feeling that's hard to describe. When you hear [A.O., A.O.] from the fans it's wonderful, but when you hear it from your teammates, it's special. They chanted quite a while. It put me on top of the world. I appreciated it very much."

—Amos Otis

Those Cheating Swine

During a game in Kansas City in the late 1970s, the Royals were playing host to the A's. By this time, the Royals had become a better team than their old rivals. No matter. It still was the A's and Royals. There was a big crowd and the atmosphere was electric.

In the top of the first inning, Oakland's Joe Rudi drilled a double into the corner. Then somebody else came up and smoked one. The next hitter, Sal Bando, hit a rocket into the alley. Wow! Three batters, three bullets! For some reason, the A's were just all over the Royals' pitcher.

Almost immediately, Whitey came out of the dugout and went up to the home plate umpire and started talking to him. We couldn't figure out what in the world was happening. Then Whitey and the home plate umpire walked down the third base line and said something to the third base umpire.

Meanwhile, we had no idea what was up. We threw out a couple possibilities. All of a sudden, it hit me, and I said on the air, "Maybe Whitey thinks they're stealing signs." And I went on to say how there could be someone in the bullpen with binoculars, looking in at the Royals' catcher and seeing what pitch he's calling. Then another guy could inconspicuously signal to the batter, such as with a towel, what pitch is coming.

I was just throwing that out as a possibility. Sure enough, Whitey and the umpires started walking toward the A's bullpen in right field. The Oakland players were seated near the fence. As Whitey and the umpires walked down the line of chairs, hmmm, there was a towel. Oops! Somebody picked it up, and there were the binoculars, which the umpire held up.

Whitey and I may have been the only two people in the stadium who had any idea what kind of shenanigans the A's were trying to pull. I was guessing … Whitey was apparently dead sure.

Here Vida, Vida, Vida

One more note on Amos Otis. The rivalry between the A's and the Royals also could be seen in one-on-one matchups. The biggest one that comes to mind was Vida Blue and A.O.

Amos was famous for wanting the umpire to look at the ball. He would do that a lot. But when Blue pitched he would do it all the time, and it would just drive Vida bonkers. In one game, Vida got so frustrated that instead of tossing the ball into the umpire, he rolled it, like a bowler, into home plate. A.O. was off to the side of home plate with a little smirk on his face, as if to say: I'm in his head good now.

"I knew from the beginning that once Vida got his rhythm going, if you didn't break it, he'd mow you down. So I'd step out and ask the umpire to check the ball. Sometimes Vida would get so frustrated that he'd throw the ball to me to check. If I didn't like it, I'd throw it out. If I was happy with it, I'd throw it back to him. Usually I threw it out. I was just doing all of that to break Vida's rhythm."

—Amos Otis

But it didn't stop with batter and pitcher. Once Amos got on base, he would continue to torment Vida. Amos could do that to several pitchers, but there was something special about the way he could get under Vida's skin. Any time Amos reached first against Vida, A.O. got the biggest lead you would ever see a major-leaguer take against a major-league pitcher. I don't know how Amos figured out that he could do it, but it was amazing. I've never seen a runner take that kind of lead at first against any pitcher in the major leagues. And it drove Vida nuts.

Remember the sliding pit at first base? That always was a good barometer on a runner's lead. If a base runner had his right foot, his front foot, on the carpet, he had a pretty big lead. Well, against Vida Blue, Amos would have both feet on the carpet, and his left foot would be a good two or three feet from the seam. He was almost to second base. Vida didn't have a good move, and Amos knew that.

Vida Blue would get so distracted by A.O. It was just hilarious.

Speaking of Brawls

The rivalries with the Rangers and White Sox didn't last long. They were more like mini-rivalries capped by a couple of fights.

The fight in Texas, actually, was huge. I believe Darrell Porter was involved in that brawl. This one was a hockey fight, unlike most baseball brawls. There was no dancing; there was only duking. That was an ugly fight.

Another big fight came in 1977 during the mini-rivalry with the White Sox. Porter and Bart Johnson got into it. Tensions were high that season, but the Royals won 102 games that year and finished ahead of second-place Chicago by eight games. Late in that season, from August 31 through a doubleheader on September 15, the Royals won a franchise-best 16 in a row. I guess all the White Sox could hope for was an on-field brawl, because they weren't going to get hold of the Royals any other way.

The Damn Yankees

The connection between Kansas City and the Yankees goes back to the 1930s and '40s, when Kansas City was a Class AAA farm club for the Yankees. Even when the A's came to Kansas City in 1955, many people thought we were still a farm team for the Yankees, because they shipped several players from K.C. to New York. The most notable was Roger Maris. I think there was a lot of resentment toward the Yankees because they took advantage of Kansas City by taking our better players.

That background didn't hurt when the Royals' rivalry with the Yankees started.

One More Fight

As with many rivalries, the one between the Royals and Yankees was based on good baseball, but very physical play. During one 1977 postseason game, George Brett tripled to center and said that as he was sliding into third, he was kicked in the face by Yankee third baseman Graig Nettles. So George came up out of his slide swinging.

As heated as the games were between the Royals and Yankees, we really didn't have that many fights. Things were pretty calm and cool.

July 24, 1983

If there was one game that was a freeze-frame from the rivalry, it would be the Pine Tar game. Just mention it and most baseball fans know exactly what you're talking about.

It was one of those games when you felt as if Brett was going to do something big.

When the Yankees were in Kansas City the week before, they had seen all the pine tar on George's bat. But they didn't do anything because no situation came up that warranted a protest. That information was catalogued, though, in their minds. Nothing happened in the first two games in New York, so manager Billy Martin just waited until the perfect time. They sat on it for five games.

In the series finale, George hit the homer off of Goose Gossage. To the Yankees' credit, they figured they had a good case for Brett to be ruled out. As we all know, home plate umpire Tim McClelland agreed with Martin and called Brett out. Eventually, the league office sided with the Royals and reversed the decision, and we had to go back to New York to finish the game.

Most people still can picture an enraged Brett charging out of the dugout toward home plate and McClelland. Brett's expression typified how all the players felt about the rivalry. I don't think any play or player could better define that rivalry than Brett's reaction.

Just Win, Baby

The mindset of the Yankees and Royals during those years was to do whatever it took to win. That is why the rivalry was so good.

The teams were competitive during the regular season and the postseason. The crowds were into it. The players definitely were into it.

Here's how I would sum up 1976, '77 and '78: The two teams were about as evenly matched as any two teams could be. The Royals were the better team in 1977, the Yankees were the better team in 1978, and the two teams were dead even in 1976. But the Yankees won all three, largely because they had a closer and the Royals didn't. The Yankees had Sparky Lyle, and the Royals didn't have a set guy. Then the Royals were better in 1980.

Even though the rivalry lasted into the 1980s, it wasn't as good as we saw it during that five-year stretch from 1976-80. Everybody remembers the playoffs, but there were some classics in the regular season.

Along Came the Cardinals

The rivalry with the Cardinals is a natural one because the teams are on opposite sides of Missouri. The Cardinals were the first major-league team to play the Royals at Municipal Stadium. They came in for a two-game exhibition series before the Twins came to town for the opener in 1969. From that quick series, I will always remember that Buddy Blattner introduced me to Tim McCarver, and he made fun of my tie. He was bigger than me, so I didn't make fun of him at all. We have laughed about that since.

Then the Royals and Cardinals would play each year in spring training in Florida.

Everything really heated up, though, during the World Series in 1985. We were lucky to see them in the World Series.

Now we get them every year during interleague play. That's been a lot of fun, but I wish we played them more often. For instance, after playing the Cardinals in a home-and-home series during 2003, the two teams met for only one series in 2004. It doesn't make a lot of sense.

Developing Rivalries

Besides the Cardinals, the Royals don't really have any rivalries going right now. The way things are structured now, it's tough to get a rivalry going.

I have said before, and authored a plan at the request of David Glass, that baseball needs to realign and do away with the American and National Leagues as we currently know them. There should be four eight-team divisions. The Royals would play primarily teams in the central time zone. That would give us natural, regional, built-in rivalries. For instance, the Cubs-White Sox; the Cubs-Cardinals would remain; the Royals-Cardinals and the Rangers-Astros would be added.

It is important for baseball to promote the rivalries that it has in place. Fans can relate to that. Among other things, rivalries between teams lessen the blow of players changing uniforms so much. If your favorite player moves to another team, you don't like it, but you still can look forward to great baseball and interesting rivalries.

Chapter
4
LEADERSHIP
AT LEVEL FIVE

The fifth floor at Kauffman Stadium houses the club's executive offices. One of the most noticeable things about the Royals as an organization is the fact that good people work for the club. Sure, there probably have been some who wouldn't fit into that mold, but most have been genuinely good people. The people within the organization are good for baseball and good for the Kansas City community.

From day one, that principle has started at the top. Ewing Kauffman, the team's original owner, knew he was running a business and understood the value of having competent people around him. From the early days of Mr. and Mrs. Kauffman, with associates such as Cedric Tallis, Lou Gorman, Joe Burke, John Schuerholz and Herk Robinson, to today with Mr. and Mrs. David Glass and associates such as Dan Glass, Allard Baird, Muzzy Jackson, Mark Gorris and Herk Robinson, this organization has been one of the best in baseball.

The following are some of Denny's recollections of the people—owners, general managers, managers and coaches—who have made the Royals organization one of the best in baseball.

Ewing Kauffman

Mr. Kauffman was not a big baseball fan, but he was the guy with the wherewithal to buy an expansion team and bring baseball back to Kansas City. As I mentioned in the first chapter, several people persuaded him to buy the club, but ultimately I think his wife Muriel pushed him over the edge. He was very conservative, and she was more outgoing.

After deciding to pursue it, Mr. Kauffman turned his attention to learning more about baseball. He decided that if he got the franchise, he was going to hire the best baseball people that he could hire, and then step back, stay out of the way and learn. He was very hands-off.

He became interested in and knowledgeable about baseball. He was a great owner, very respected by the other owners.

The Right Man at the Right Time

Ewing Kauffman may have been one of the best owners in the history of baseball. He put his money into it and let his people make the decisions, and he pretty much let those people do what they thought they needed to do to win. As Ewing progressed in his ownership tenure, there were times when he needed to be more involved, so he was. Otherwise, we didn't see him very often.

"[Early in the club's history] I remember doing P.R. tours during the winter with pitcher Tom Burgmeier, going to towns all around the Midwest. The Royals hired players for the entire off-season to go out there for three or four months on a personal basis. It was Mr. Kauffman's idea for season-ticket selling exposure to the six states that they were trying to reach. In the mornings, Tom and I would get up with farmers and go hunting on their farms. And then we'd leave tickets for them during the season. It was a neat arrangement."

—Joe Keough

A Smart Owner

Owning the club was good for Ewing, and he was smart enough to realize that he was getting into a business that he did not really know much about. That's the reason he hired Cedric Tallis and Lou Gorman, who, in turn, hired John Schuerholz and Herk Robinson.

Ewing put those people in place and simply let them run the business. He had final approval over everything, obviously, but he let the baseball people do their thing. It was largely due to that willingness to get baseball people that the team prospered so quickly.

"I have so many wonderful memories of working with the Royals: The opportunity to work for Ewing Kauffman, a man who put his heart and soul into bringing major league baseball back to Kansas City after Charlie Finley took the team to Oakland, is first. The chance to work with him and the wonderful people who were businessmen and women who committed themselves as Royal Lancers to create a volunteer sales force to generate sales and enthusiasm in the community. The organization was the best it could be from 1976, when we won our first division, to 1985 when we won our world championship. We had a lot of fun. The organization was born in Kansas City; we grew up there and we matured there as an organization. The tone was set by Mr. Kauffman. It was a thrill and an honor to work for the man."

—*John Schuerholz*

Always Thinking of Others

Mr. K was very loyal, and he expected loyalty in return. That was high on his priority list. He gave and wanted back. That's one of the few things he wanted from the people around him: loyalty and dedication to what they were doing. If he knew he had that and knew they were productive, he would leave them alone. Then, in return, he would take care of those people in a lot of ways. So it was a good reciprocal deal.

The last time I saw Ewing was about three weeks before he died. He was at the stadium in a suite by himself, so I went in and sat with him for about 15 or 20 minutes. We just chatted. We didn't really talk about anything specific; it was just a situation, like the others as we got to know each other, in which we talked about different things such as the club, baseball and investing.

Ewing was very good about getting all his Royals ("associates" as he liked to call them) and everyone who worked for him, and saying, "We've got a lot of investment people now, and we want you to save your money and make good decisions with your money."

The Royals' first first-family. Owner Ewing Kauffman and his wife, Muriel. This was at Game 1 of the 1985 American League playoffs in Toronto. Mrs. K was a native of Toronto. *Photo courtesy of the Kansas City Royals*

He encouraged all of us to tap his investment people. He'd say, "You go in there and see them." He was just like a father. It was obvious how much he really cared.

He wanted to make sure that he could make as many people as possible happy and comfortable, but he would not give anyone anything. That is best summed up in a story he used to tell when he would say, "When I see a guy, a beggar, along the street and the guy asks me for food, I won't give him fish. I'll give him a fishing pole."

A Fun First Lady

Ewing and Muriel Kauffman were great together, a terrific pair. He was a businessman; she was a lawyer.

I remember when Mrs. K decided that she would become Ewing's wardrobe consultant. She started buying him these Royal blue suits.

People were drawn to Muriel. She was a very outgoing, gregarious, fun-loving person. He was early to bed, early to rise, and she was late to bed, a party-goer. He would hang with her about 20 minutes, and then she would grab 17 other people and they'd stay out until two in the morning, just having a good time.

"The old guy is going to bed," she would say, "so I'm going to go out to party." And she would. She was a person with whom I felt comfortable from the beginning.

David Glass

David Glass became the Royals' owner and CEO on April 18, 2000. David grew up in Mountain View, Missouri, and graduated from Southwest Missouri State in Springfield.

Our backgrounds are somewhat similar—we both grew up loyal Cardinals fans, listening to Harry Caray and Jack Buck on the vast Cardinals Radio Network. We have always enjoyed talking about Cardinal players of the late 1950s and '60s, and we both experienced our first big-league baseball games at the old Busch Stadium/Sportsman's Park in St. Louis.

David became a recognizable figure in business as the President and CEO of Wal-Mart. He climbed up the ladder at Wal-Mart, starting with the company in 1976 as Executive Vice President of Finance, before retiring as CEO in January 2000.

Ewing Kauffman liked the fact that he and David shared similar Midwestern values. In fact, you had the feeling that if Mr. Kauffman could pick one person to own the team after him, it would be David Glass.

Ewing was confident that if David acquired the club, he would have a similar business philosophy and would run the ball club in a way that best served the organization and the baseball fans of Kansas City.

During the succession period between Mr. K's passing and David buying the club, there was a board of directors that ran the organization. Beginning in 1993, David was the chairman of the board, Mike Herman was the president, and Herk Robinson was the general manager. They were the primary figures who guided the Royals through that important and sometimes difficult transition.

The first time I met David Glass was in the press club at the ballpark during the season. Herk was taking David around and introducing him to as many people as he could. From the moment I met him, I liked him. I had the feeling that we connected. He's so easy-going and friendly that I felt we'd get along. And we have.

A couple times a year we get together for lunch, and it's always intriguing to sit down with him and discuss everything from baseball to world events. Baseball discussion covers about 80 percent of lunch, but we find time to work in some other topics.

And Now the Voice of the Royals, David Glass

Once in a while, David will pop into the booth during a game, and it's always fun having him on the air. In one of his early visits to the booth in spring training after he had purchased the club, toward the end of our chat on the air, I half-kiddingly asked him if on his next visit to the booth, he'd like to do an inning or two of play-by-play. He grinned broadly and said, "Sure! I can do that."

I was slightly taken aback by the answer. But with his background, interest and knowledge of the game, it occurred to me that if he did an inning or two on the radio, he quite likely would do it so well and enjoy it so much that my play-by-play innings would be cut back drastically. Luckily for me, with all of David's Wal-Mart and Royals obligations,

Royals owner David Glass with his wife Ruth and yours truly in June 1995. I hope Royals fans appreciate the Glass family's desire to have a winning franchise in Kansas City. *Photo courtesy of Denny Matthews*

time has not allowed him to join the ranks of the play-by-play announcers.

Dan Glass

Many outsiders might want to scoff at the idea that David's son, Dan, is the president of the Royals. Spend any time with Dan, however, and you'll quickly realize that he's earned his position on his merits and not on his name.

Like his dad, Dan Glass grew up with a love of baseball and, in particular, the St. Louis Cardinals. He had acquired a lot of Cardinal memorabilia, which I also had done, so we enjoyed comparing notes and reminiscing about some of the great Redbirds.

That love of baseball and a strong work ethic helped give Dan the knowledge he needed to effectively guide the organization. Dan's experience in baseball came through grass-roots work. From 1993-98, Dan worked in the Royals' baseball operations department. He started as the baseball operations assistant before becoming the assistant director of player personnel in 1996. He has been active in player development and scouting for the Royals, including the development and coordination of the Royals' Latin America program.

He was appointed Royals president in 2000 and has done a terrific job of emphasizing a family atmosphere throughout the organization and charting a course for future success. By installing competent people in all departments, he has positioned the Royals to be competitive on the field and at the box office. The Royals' improvement in 2003 and the excitement generated by the team confirm that the Royals, indeed, are headed in a proper direction.

Leading One Link at a Time

Although Dan doesn't get to spend as much time as he would like on golf, he is a very competent linkster. In fact, he has the distinction of holing one of the longest putts in the history of the Wolf Creek Golf Club.

He and I were playing out there in November 2002, and on the No. 14 hole, we both found ourselves with long, twisting putts. Truth be known, we both barely made it on the green. He stroked about an 85-

foot, twisting, rolling putt that went right into the hole. We both almost fell into the pond in front of the green. My upcoming putt was roughly five feet shorter on exactly the same line. I figured if Dan was president of the Royals, and the leader, that I should follow suit. Yep, you guessed it. I drained my putt. What were the odds? I'll let him line up my putts anytime!

THE GENERAL MANAGERS

Cedric Tallis

Cedric was with the Angels as director of stadium operations when the Royals hired him. Cedric and Buddy Blattner were good friends while both were with the Angels. Cedric was a big, gruff bear of a man. He was a little intimidating physically. And as I recall, he was an officer during World War II. He had a bit of a military presence about him.

The other side of Cedric was a very kind, thoughtful and a good-hearted guy. He had a good sense of humor. We had the feeling that he had a good vision and plan for the expansion team; he knew what he wanted to get done. As I mentioned earlier, he made some fantastic trades that really built the ball club's strength in a hurry.

"Cedric certainly was a character. We became friends while we both were with the Angels. In fact, he's one of the main reasons I joined the Royals. It is very important that a GM be popular among other general managers; they almost have their own club. Cedric was very, very popular. We were an expansion club, and Cedric could make deals that other GMs could not. He also was very astute. Cedric was liked by the ballplayers, the managers, and the coaches. He was fun to be around. He was a terrible driver—he would go 90 miles per hour in a 10 miles-per-hour zone. Working for the Yankees, he was one of the few men I know to stand up to George Steinbrenner. Overall, Cedric simply enjoyed life to the fullest."

—Buddy Blattner

Fred Astaire Would Be Proud
(Or If Not, Danny Terrio Would)

After a few drinks and a good dinner, Cedric fancied himself a good dancer. One night during spring training, we had about 18 people at the Ft. Myers Country Club for dinner. As soon as the first note cranked out of the band, Cedric's ears and eyes perked up and he was on the dance floor. He would dance with anybody.

The big bear was pretty light on his feet. He loved to whirl and twirl, spin and dip; he had all the moves. Woe to the partner who couldn't keep up with him. More than one lady went meandering off the dance floor, not knowing where the whirlwind had come from.

It got to be pretty late this particular night, and Cedric was dancing with a woman. At the end of this number, Cedric did his spinout move with a little more enthusiasm, power, and exuberance than usual. He whirled his partner around; she lost her balance and went flying down the table. As she went flying, so did the tablecloth, glasses, napkins, and people. It was quite a finale.

A New Trick from the Food Channel

During spring training, Cedric rented a condominium in Florida. He often went out with the ladies from the office or invited them to the condo for dinner. This one particular night, he invited them over for dinner to his place. When they got there, he had a beautiful spread with a perfectly green salad, fantastic fresh fruit, succulent corn on the cob and incredible steaks. Everything was perfect. Cedric offered the ladies a drink, and they sat back and watched the master chef at work. The final touch, "Ladies, how would you like your steaks?"

Peggy Mathews said, "Medium."

Bev Tierney said, "Make mine medium well."

With that Cedric said, "Very well," picked up the three beautiful steaks, and dropped them into a pot of boiling water.

What a memorable meal—salad, fruit, corn on the cob and parboiled catcher's glove.

Joe Burke

Joe Burke worked in Louisville (Kentucky) with a farm team there. Eventually, he made it to Washington, where he worked for the Senators. Joe was on the business side more than the baseball side. He loved baseball, but he was more of a business guy. He turned to the baseball side more in Texas with the Rangers.

Joe came to the Royals in 1973 and became the general manager in 1974. He made some pretty good trades with the Royals, including the Darrell Porter deal in December 1976 that sent Jamie Quirk, Jim Wohlford and Bob McClure to Milwaukee. He proved to be solid as a general manager, even though he was conservative.

Joe was a very religious man. He had a large family, and a couple of his boys still live in the Kansas City area. Joe Burke was about as straight and moral an individual as you'd want to meet. He had a very good outlook on life. If somebody was having some problems, they could go to Joe's office and they'd come out feeling pretty good. It would be hard not to like Joe.

Joe lost his battle with cancer in 1992.

John Schuerholz

John Schuerholz grew up in the Baltimore area. He played baseball and soccer collegiately at Towson State. When he graduated from college, he became a schoolteacher. He always had a love of baseball and the Orioles. John's very outgoing, glib, a good conversationalist. John was fun to be around. He has a quick wit; he's humorous and full of life. While teaching, he was intrigued by baseball as a career. He wrote a letter to the Baltimore Orioles, and it got into the hands of Lou Gorman, who was the head of the scouting department. Lou needed an assistant in his office, so he interviewed John. Thus began John's baseball career.

Not long thereafter, two or three years later, Lou came to the Royals to lead the scouting department. They both ended up here with the Royals in 1968 as two of the first hires by general manager Cedric Tallis. In the fall of 1969, Herk Robinson was hired. The three of them worked together and had a great relationship.

Lou eventually left the Royals, while John and Herk stayed. A few years later, in October 1981, John became the general manager, replacing Joe Burke, who became the team's president.

"I learned what I know from John Schuerholz. I started with the Royals in 1976 as John's assistant. I fell into a pretty good situation. I didn't realize what a good situation until I look back now. You don't appreciate what a good man Mr. Kauffman was until you have to work with some of these other people around the league. I was a low-level guy and didn't have much interaction with Mr. Kauffman until my later years with the organization. I became involved in several meetings, and he always was a very laid-back man, but a very astute man. He hired great baseball people to run his organization. As long as he was informed about what was going on, he let you do your job."

—Dick Balderson, who left the Royals to become
the GM of the Seattle Mariners

John, of course, was the general manager when the Royals won the World Series in 1985. The young pitching staff was coming into its own at that time.

Interestingly, he went to Atlanta and built their pitching staff with young talent. The Braves had been horrible for years, and John built them into a champion. They've stayed toward the top for years and years, which is quite an achievement.

The Schuerholz Twins... or the Matthews Twins...

During spring training in 1969, the first one for the club, nobody really knew anybody. People were wandering around trying to figure out who was who. John and I are the same age, basically the same build, same hair color. We didn't look unlike each other. For that first week of spring training, nearly every day, people were coming up to me asking me about meal money, minor league assignments, minor league affiliates, etc. Being young and in my first major league camp, I figured I was supposed to know, so I answered their questions as best as I could. Meanwhile, guys were going up to John and asking him about interviews and how large the radio network was going to be. John figured that was supposed to be something he should know, so he BSed his way through that.

Finally a light came on one day when we were talking … people were getting us confused.

So we made a pact at that point in time. I tried to give him as many answers as I could about what he was being asked, and he did likewise for me. We figured in the interest of time saved and BS being rendered, we would have the answers and neither John nor I cared that people thought we were the other. Hopefully after 35 years, most people can tell us apart.

Herk Robinson

Spencer "Herk" Robinson grew up in St. Louis. He loved the game of baseball. Unlike so many St. Louis fans, he wasn't a fan of the Cardinals. He was a fan of the Browns. He was a "member" of the Knothole Gang. (I don't know how many young Browns fans there were, but I'm guessing that he didn't have to stand in line long to get a look through the fence.)

Bill DeWitt was running the Browns at that time. Bill DeWitt Jr. and Herk were boyhood friends. DeWitt Sr. bought the Cincinnati Reds. Despite the DeWitts' move east, Herk and Bill Jr. kept their friendship. When Herk was 13 or 14 years old, he had a chance to go to spring training with Bill Jr. They did odd jobs together around the ballpark. But in essence, that was when his baseball career started. That's when he decided that he wanted to spend his life in baseball. His first full-time job ended up being with the Reds in scouting. What a background!

Herk joined the Royals in the winter after the 1969 season. He worked side by side with John Schuerholz under Lou Gorman.

In 1973, Herk had a choice: to stay on the baseball side or become the vice president in charge of stadium operations. The decision hinged on the fact that his two daughters were young and he wanted to be at home to help raise them. Herk's a handyman, so a position in stadium operations was a perfect fit for him. His role was expanded through the years until he became general manager in 1990. But the way the stadium looks today is a tribute to Herk's 17 years overseeing it.

Herk became the GM when John went to Atlanta. People thought the Royals were crazy selecting Herk as general manager. People overlooked the fact that Herk's background was in scouting and player development. In fact, he may have had more experience than John in those areas. Obviously those doubtful thoughts were unfounded.

Herk had a great relationship with Mr. Kauffman. As Mr. K did with all of his general managers, he gave Herk free rein to do what he needed to do to make the team competitive, within financial reason. Herk had been GM for only a couple of years before Mr. K passed away. So suddenly, instead of dealing with only one person, Mr. Kauffman, Herk was dealing with a board of directors. To me, Herk did a great job, given the circumstances and parameters under which he had to work.

Herk's a very serious, dedicated, loyal, honest individual. He's a great father and husband to his family.

The Green Thumb

Herk's father was an expert gardener. Herk gained his father's love of all things green. Even if he isn't licensed as such, Herk is a leading authority on lawns, grasses, trees, even weeds … all things growing.

Herk and his wife, Kathy, moved frequently during the late 1970s and '80s. Needless to say, wherever he's lived, Herk's had the most impeccably groomed landscape. The grass is always greener, the trees are strong and healthy, everything is perfectly trimmed.

Whenever Herk and Kathy moved, and I would go to the new house, I would simply ask Herk in which neighborhood he was living. I knew I could drive through that neighborhood until I found a house with perfect landscaping and the greenest grass and simply pull into that driveway. That's obviously where Herk and Kathy lived.

Allard Baird

Allard Baird grew up in New Hampshire. I remember him telling me a story about, as a very young guy, going to Fenway Park and seeing the Boston Red Sox. He said that day he was taken by the very spectacle of baseball. It was evident from that day that Allard Baird was going to be a baseball guy.

As a kid, he played the game. He was a middle infielder. He then became a coach at Broward Community College in Florida in 1986. He had been a coach at Southern Arkansas University, which also is where he played collegiately. He owned and operated a baseball school in Ft. Lauderdale from 1986-93.

The first scouting department. (Back row, from left) Al Diaz, Art Lilly, Rosey Gilhousen, Art Stewart, Bill Fischer and Gary Blalock. (Front row, from left) Syd Thrift, John Schuerholz, Lou Gorman, Tom Ferrick. *Photo courtesy of the Kansas City Royals*

In 1988, Allard joined the Royals as a hitting instructor at Class A Appleton (Wisconsin). In 1990 he went from coaching to scouting, becoming a territorial scout for the Royals. Then, in 1993, he was promoted to national cross-checker. That meant that if the Royals considered making a trade, Allard would go see the players involved in the potential deal. In February 1997, he became a special assistant to Herk. At that time, Herk was grooming Allard to take over for him at some point.

Allard is a tireless worker. His one speed is all out. He is intellectually aggressive. From his days as a scout, he's very detail-oriented. Nothing escapes him. He has hired good people, so he has an excellent core around him. But he's very much hands-on. He doesn't ask someone to go watch a player; usually he goes.

Most scouts can readily evaluate physical skills. What separates Allard is his ability to evaluate the intangibles (the player's character, background, feel for the game, competitiveness, and heart). It isn't necessarily the physical skills that allow a player to reach the big leagues and be productive; it is the combination of physical ability combined with all of those important intangibles.

Allard already has made some excellent moves as Royals general manager. His future as a baseball administrator is extremely bright.

Lou Gorman

Even though Lou Gorman wasn't a general manager with the Royals, he worked closely with the first two general managers and groomed two—John Schuerholz and Herk Robinson—who became general managers. After leaving the Royals, Lou became a general manager for Boston and Seattle.

James Lou Gorman was the quintessential New England gentleman. He was unfailingly polite and friendly, prim and proper on all occasions, in any environment. Lou was extremely intelligent, a compelling conversationalist, a lover of good food and a master at the malapropism.

At times, Lou would get so excited and enthusiastic about something (usually baseball) that his words would run together and not come out in quite the proper order or in the way in which they were intended. Some of his malapropisms (a humorous misuse of a word or phrase) are priceless.

To many who knew and loved Lou, his malapropisms became known as "Gormanisms." John and Herk kept a list of them, which, of course, they kept hidden in their desks. Here are some of the best of the best.

One day in the 1970s, he had heard about a high school pitcher with a phenomenal arm and reputation. Lou wanted to fly out and see the pitcher as soon as he could. He went flying into the office of his assistant, Nancy Gaba, and promptly asked her to "book me in an airport near a hotel."

One day he was asked about a prospect in the Royals organization. He promptly replied: "I think he'll be fine once he figures out which side of the street his bread is buttered on."

One year, when they were getting down to placing players at the end of spring training, they had scouting reports and stats and a photo in front of him. Lou couldn't make the decision about one guy, Joel Bishop. Lou said, "We were faced face to face with the face of Joel Bishop."

Some other classic Gormanisms:

"We're going to have to start eating the meal money."
"If it gets any warmer, that plant will start hibernation."
"That car burns gas like it's eating peanuts."
"Put a gun to his head and blow the trigger off."
"I'll keep my ears posted."
"I vaguely and vividly remember in my own mind."
"He looks like a rug carpet salesman."
"Get Kirkpatrick's back in there."
"We're glad to have you with you."
"My car spurt and bumped from the dealer."
"You've got a woman gal pumping gas now."
"Hasbach's leg is just out of the crutch."
"He looked like he threw real good just listening on the radio."
"Eddie Sawyer has a store he owns some money in."
"We had a meeting with budget and Burke and Kauffman."
"I hadn't even met her name yet."
"I'll have a dark meatball sandwich."
"Do you have Tom's residence right now where he is?"
"It has real high ceilings covered with paintings and tapestries." (Interesting ceiling.)

"The toe nail on the top toe is growing into the nail." (Sounds painful.)

THE MANAGERS

Joe Gordon

Joe Gordon was a terrific second baseman as a player. As a manager, he was happy-go-lucky and very friendly, with a great sense of humor. Joe was a bright guy who loved word games.

General manager Cedric Tallis hired Joe as the team's first manager, figuring Joe would be perfect for a young expansion club because he was a low-pressure guy. Joe really didn't want to manage. He was happy, enjoying retirement, but he did it as a favor to Cedric. He managed here only in the 1969 season. The players loved him, and he did a good job in the organization's first year.

Charlie Metro

Charlie Metro was a taskmaster. I think he might have been a little too stern with the young team. He was an old-school, all-business baseball guy. He was a part of the Chicago Cubs "college of coaches," the one season they utilized eight or 10 coaches, each taking turns at being manager, instead of hiring a full-time manager.

Charlie loved Western art and Western stories. He loved horses. I liked Charlie—he was smart and an engaging conversationalist.

Bob Lemon

Bob Lemon was very much like Joe Gordon, one of his friends. Lem was a good guy, and everybody liked playing for him. Bob's

Manager Bob Lemon (top left) and his coaching staff at spring training: (clockwise from top right) Joe Schultz, Dan Carnevale, Charlie Metro and Harry Dunlop. *Photo courtesy of the Kansas City Royals*

nickname for everybody was "meat." He knew people's names, but he insisted on calling everyone meat.

"I'll always remember Bob Lemon, because he's the one who really got me over the hump. Before him, I kept going from the minors to the majors and back down again. When I got to Kansas City, he called me into his office during my first spring training with the Royals [in 1972]. He said, 'John, the job [at first] is yours if you can prove that you can do it.' That's all I needed to hear. I've never heard any of the guys say anything bad about Bob Lemon. He was a baseball man to the full degree."

—John Mayberry

Lem had a favorite restaurant in Milwaukee where he loved to eat. It was a German place called Carl Ratsch's. Steve Cameron, who was writing with the *Topeka Capital Journal*, was invited with a few of us to go to Carl's for dinner. (Steve, by the way, was growing a beard, and Lem loved to get on him about it.) Steve had a deadline for an article, and he knew that he had to get back to the hotel before 10:30 to finish it that night.

After dinner, Lemon suggested that we go to the bar and have an after-dinner drink. We started drinking a German gin, which you're supposed to sip. It was strong stuff. Lem warned Steve that he couldn't slam it down. Steve was confident that he could. So Lem bet Steve $20 that he couldn't (and shouldn't) slam it down. Of course, Steve accepted the bet and slammed down the drink. Suddenly, it looked as if his eyes were on fire, and he got a goofy look on his face. He didn't know whether to throw up, pass out, or simply explode.

Steve had a couple more shots, and then suddenly looked at his watch to discover it was 10:15. He excused himself and wobbled out of the bar, certainly not looking like a reporter on deadline. And we pick up the story now with what Steve told me the next day.

"I got back to my room, turned on the TV to find *The Tonight Show* just starting. I put some paper in my typewriter and sat down on the edge of the bed, thinking about my story. The next thing I remember, my eyes opened, it was daylight, the lights and the TV were still glowing and the clock read 9:45 a.m."

When Steve got to the ballpark that day, Lem saw Cameron in his still weakened condition. Lem got a little smile on his face and said to Steve, "I hope you had a good time last night. And, by the way, meat, you don't have to worry about your beard any more ... it's gone." The beard was still there, of course, but like Steve, it was in need of further repair.

Whitey Herzog

Whitey Herzog was Jack McKeon's successor in 1975. Whitey infused a great spirit and confidence into the team that they were lacking. He really pushed the young guys like Frank White, Al Cowens, George Brett, and Willie Wilson. He was a great manager for young guys. He would challenge and prod them sometimes. He had a good knack of knowing which guys needed a swift kick and which guys needed a pat on the back. And some of them needed both from time to time. His timing and judgment were very good in that regard.

"I stepped into the Royals job at a wonderful time. George Brett was a rookie having a tremendous year. John Mayberry hit 34 home runs that season. Frank White and Al Cowens were on the bench, so I put both of them in the lineup, which was like making a major trade to get two stars without giving up anybody. White became an outstanding second baseman. Freddie Patek at shortstop was a tremendous player. With Mayberry, White, Patek and Brett on the infield, we really had a great infield. Then, Cowens became an All-Star in right field; Amos Otis was an All-Star in center; then our left fielders of Tom Poquette, Jim Wohlford, and Joe Zdeb did a super job.

"To me, the biggest acquisition at that time was getting Darrell Porter before the 1977 season in a trade with Milwaukee. He was a tremendous ballplayer for us. Not only did he throw everybody out at catcher, he was a tough out at the plate. He did a lot of things on the ball field to help us win that the average fan didn't notice."

—*Whitey Herzog*

He had a great knack for making the last guys on the roster feel like they were as important as anyone in the regular lineup. He would give the guys on the bench playing time, while giving his regulars rest. He was very good at balancing that out. No players on the team, regardless of position, were forgotten by Whitey. He made a point to talk personally with one or two different players each day.

We Don't Really Need the Starters

Whitey managed the Royals to the greatest comeback in the club's history. It was on Friday night, June 15, 1979, at Milwaukee. We had a day game scheduled for Saturday afternoon.

By about the fourth inning, the Royals were trailing by a ton of runs. They eventually went down by an 11-2 score. So Whitey took his starters out of the lineup and told them to go back to the hotel and get a good night's sleep: "We'll get 'em tomorrow afternoon."

As it turned out, the subs rallied, made up the nine-run difference with three more, and won 14-11.

Taping the *Whitey Herzog Show* in 1978. One night I asked Whitey to compare the two starting pitchers, and he said, "They're similar in a lot of different ways."
Photo courtesy of Denny Matthews

There was a lounge right off the main lobby at our hotel, the Pfister. When we got back there after the game, around 11 p.m., the guys who went back early to get a good night's sleep were sitting in the lounge swapping stories. As we entered the hotel, one of the guys getting off the bus announced: "We don't need you guys; we won."

It took a lot of convincing before those guys believed they actually missed the greatest comeback in club history.

The Wit and Wisdom of the White Rat

Whitey Herzog had some great comments during his pregame show that would really startle me. Sometimes they aired; sometimes they didn't.

One night when the team hadn't been playing well, in his best Casey Stengel truism (he didn't do it on purpose) he said, "Yeah, we haven't been playing very well, but you're only as good as you are, and you can't do what you can't do."

Whitey had a couple of other theorems I loved. One was, "It's hard to be lucky when you're horse s---." That pretty much applies to everything, doesn't it? The other one that I always liked, and always favored as a broadcaster, was when he once said, "If you're going to play horse s---, play fast." I really liked that one.

Yep, the wit and wisdom of "The White Rat."

A Conflict of Interest

Whitey immediately recognized the talent that he had. He also realized that in Royals Stadium, then the biggest ballpark along with St. Louis, he needed speed and defense to win. So, wanting to put pressure on the opposing defense, he got a running team.

However, Whitey was very aggressive and always wanted to change things. General manager Joe Burke was very conservative. So those two styles clashed to a degree. I think Whitey just kept pushing and pushing and he fell out of favor. When he was fired after the 1979 season, it was not a popular decision among fans. The Royals, though, felt they needed a change, based more on a personality conflict than anything else.

Jim Frey

Jim Frey was a coach in Baltimore under Earl Weaver for years and years. How much of Earl rubbed off on Jim, I don't know, but I'm sure some. He obviously knew the game well, and he managed well, leading the club to its first ever World Series appearance in 1980.

Away from the field, he is one of the best and funniest storytellers I've ever been around. He could tell a story like nobody.

Jim Frey and John Schuerholz had known each other when they were in Baltimore. So, one night when we were there playing the Orioles, Jim, John, Fred White, and I went to this little bar in the suburbs that they liked. One of the bartenders at this place doubled as a magician … or maybe the magician doubled as one of the bartenders, I'm not sure.

Regardless, the magician/bartender would do tricks, and he was exceptionally good. The funny thing about it was that Jim had been to this place enough to know what trick the guy was performing. So when he came close to the end, Jim would start laughing. That was fun to watch.

Jim Frey loved to laugh, but it's a shame that didn't come out more on the field.
Photo courtesy of the Kansas City Royals

When we started to leave, the magician-bartender asked me if I had everything. I thought I did. "Do you want your watch back?" he asked. I looked at my wrist, and sure enough, there was no watch. That was unbelievable. That was one of my favorite nights after a game of all time.

Time for a Change

The first two months of the manager's show in 1980, when Jim started, were horrid. He was awful. He would not say anything and he didn't have a good feel for what we were doing. Then, all of a sudden, it was as if a light went on and he realized it was the *Jim Frey Show*. He went from being the worst manager on his radio show to maybe the best. He was terrific.

Jim was a fun guy to be around off the field, but at the ballpark, he was sometimes too serious. He had a great personality, but his personality away from the ballpark and at the ballpark was different. His old-school style at the park rankled some of the guys. I think people in the front office realized that Jim was losing touch with the players. I'm not exactly sure, though, because I tried to stay away from the situation.

Dick Howser

Dick Howser, who spent his rookie season as a player with the Kansas City A's, succeeded Frey during the 1981 season. Dick was a coach with the Yankees when he was hired here. He was businesslike, conservative and reserved. He wanted a set lineup with his regulars playing almost every day, and he wouldn't deviate from it. He expected his guys to know what they were supposed to do. Dick wouldn't often ask guys to do something they couldn't do.

"Dick didn't say a lot; he just expected us to work hard. His famous words when we got down were: 'Just get it done.'"

—John Wathan

"I played for some good managers, but Dick was great. He was so honest with you. If you messed around or did something wrong, he was in your face. But he allowed you to play if you were out there and ready, and he

knew you were going to give your best. That's what he was all about. If you had a bad game, he'd say that he put you in position to have a bad game; not that you had a bad game. He was a confidence-builder.

"He demanded a huge amount of respect, also. You weren't going to flip him the ball as you were walking off the mound, because you knew that if you did that, you'd never pitch again in a Royals uniform. He demanded respect, but you always knew where he stood and that he was always going to protect you. You can't ask for more out of a manager."

—*Mark Gubicza*

Dick was a fun guy away from the ballpark. He loved to play golf, but he had the goofiest golf swing I ever did see. It was like a hockey slap shot. But it worked because he was a good golfer and athlete.

Howser had a good sense of humor, but you didn't see it all that often at the ballpark. He didn't put it on display in a uniform. He was a little tough to work with on the manager's show because he was very cautious. He would give me the obvious, but that was about it because he didn't want to give away too much.

The Loss of a Great Manager

Dealing with Dick's final days in Ft. Myers before losing his battle with brain cancer was extremely difficult. It was the toughest thing I've dealt with as a broadcaster.

Dick "officially" managed the Royals until February 23, 1987. He passed away nearly four months later, on June 17.

Because of our interaction, I might have been one of the first ones to realize there was something wrong. Even though he usually wouldn't give away much on his radio show, he was very sharp. Around the middle of June in 1986, we would be taping the show and he would not recall something that happened the night before, or he would mix up names. I thought he also looked kind of tired.

As we drew closer to the All-Star break, he was having more trouble doing the show. During the break, I think, was when they found the tumor. Then, it all began to tie together.

"A lot of people talk about how different clubs have moved forward through adversity, but Dick meant so much to this club. When we got the news after the All-Star break, it was devastating. He was our leader; he was the guy who always showed confidence in us and took the heat for us no matter how bad of a game we had or how good of a game we had. It was emotional, but everyone kept it inside. Not having your general there, I think it really hurt us. We had some good clubs after 1985, but he meant so much to the organization. He was the calming influence between what happened in 1983 to us young guys coming up in 1984 to winning in 1985."

— *Mark Gubicza*

The Royals left Dick with some hope, however. Even though it could be assumed by most that the cancer would take his life sooner than later, the Royals did not hire a full-time manager. Mike Ferraro took over the team on an interim basis after the 1986 All-Star break.

That experience was difficult for everyone to handle.

John Wathan

Duke was being groomed as a future manager when Dick got sick. During Dick's illness, Wathan coached a little with the big-league club, but he also managed in Omaha. He was just starting to figure out how to manage, and boom, he's in the big leagues.

It was triple jeopardy for Wathan: he was succeeding a successful manager in the toughest of circumstances, he was still trying to figure out how he wanted to manage, and he was managing guys he played with. All of those things were working against him. But he did a superb job of overcoming those difficulties.

Wathan has done everything possible in the Royals organization: player, coach, manager, broadcaster and scout. He was a natural as a manager, with his personality and insight into the game, having played so many positions.

Duke, Does Dusty Always Stagger?

Duke had great parties out at his house in Blue Springs, Missouri. Oftentimes those parties included some touch football. In fact, Duke bought two lots, so he could have his house on one and leave the other as a big lot to play in.

One time, we were playing eight-on-eight touch football, with Bret Saberhagen, George Brett, Jamie Quirk, and a bunch of other guys. John's sons, Dusty and Derek, also were playing. Without seeing me, Saberhagen threw a pass to Dusty, and I stepped in front of it. I intercepted the pass, and as I remember it, Dusty ran into me. It was a monumental collision; it was a noisy thud. Dusty went down, and it staggered me.

I was thinking, "Oh no! I just killed Duke's son!" Oh man, I get invited to come out and play touch football and wipe out one of his offspring. Duke and I will be friends no longer. But, hey, it wasn't my fault; I never did see him.

Luckily, Dusty was a pretty big kid, and he bounced back up and shook the cobwebs from his head. And the game continued.

Hal McRae

When John Schuerholz left to take the job in Atlanta, and the 1991 season didn't get off to a fast start, new general manager Herk Robinson wanted to make a change. So Herk persuaded Hal McRae, whom he had signed as a player in Cincinnati, to take over the ball club.

"His heart had been in hitting, and he was doing well in Montreal. Hal had tremendous pride. He never wanted to embarrass himself or hurt his professionalism. But I thought he had the leadership qualities and obviously the baseball knowledge to manage the Royals. One of the biggest mistakes I ever made was terminating Hal McRae."

—*Herk Robinson*

Herk really had to do a selling job on him, because I think in Mac's mind, he wondered whether he was ready to manage. Even though he probably felt he could do it—but having not managed and being very content as the hitting coach with Montreal—Herk had to do a good selling job to convince Mac that he was the guy to manage the Royals.

Despite the lack of managerial experience, the big thing Mac had was a wonderful feel for the game of baseball. He had great insight, was a smart man, and was calculating and shrewd. He was very much in the learning process throughout his managerial career with the Royals.

Mac managed right up until the player's strike in 1994, which wiped out the rest of the season, and then he was fired in the off season. I never heard, or really ever sought, a reason why he was let go. At that point, though, there was a feeling that he was really getting a good feel for managing. In fact, the Royals had won 14 games in a row going into the strike (the club's second longest winning streak). So you could see the evolution of a big-league manager right before your eyes.

I'm not so sure he liked managing that much for the first few months, when he started in 1991. But then he turned the corner where

Hal McRae and I talk things over after he announced his retirement as an active player in October 1987. He would become Royals manager four years later.
Photo courtesy of Denny Matthews

he felt like he had a good handle on managing in the big leagues, and he was starting to enjoy it. In my estimation, he was becoming really good.

Mac said some of the most interesting things during his manager's show. Often, I walked away saying, "Man, I never would've looked at it that way, and I don't know if many people had." Mac, who was a great player's manager, wasn't afraid to say things. He gave great insight every night.

Tony Muser

I liked Tony Muser very much. We got to know each other well through the years. We had a great rapport. I considered him a good friend, and I supported him.

Tony was old-school, from a military background, so it was all business once he got to the ballpark. He was a very funny guy, and a

great storyteller, but he wouldn't let much of that come out in his dealings in uniform as manager. I always felt that if his personality and his storytelling ability and his humor would've come out more for the players, they would have been a little more loose and responsive.

He was a very solid baseball strategy guy. He was not a great player, but he worked hard.

Taping the *Tony Muser Show* with the Royals manager. Tony always had something interesting to say. We usually had a good laugh or two when the microphone was off. *Photo courtesy of Denny Matthews*

He didn't tolerate mistakes as a manager. He wanted the game played fundamentally and soundly, for which you can't blame him. To be fair, while Tony was here, the Royals didn't have any pitching. The rotation was awful and the bullpen was just OK. A lot of guys, though, such as Johnny Damon and Jermaine Dye, became very good major league players under Tony Muser.

THE COACHES

Galen Cisco, Pitching Coach

Galen "Grump" Cisco was a former football player under Woody Hayes at Ohio State. He was quiet and talked slowly. He had two sons, Jeff and Chip, one of whom played football at Ohio State and the other was a ball boy at Royals Stadium.

Away from the field, Galen was the nicest guy in the world, with a great sense of humor. As a player and coach, however, he had acquired the nickname Grump. On the field he always had a stern and businesslike look on his face. Evidently, some of Woody Hayes had rubbed off, and in uniform, Galen was dead serious, expecting players to do their jobs without flamboyance or calling attention to themselves.

Chip was about 12 years old at the time. One night, a player hit a bullet foul down the left field line. Chip came off his stool and made a great diving catch. The crowd erupted. It really was a great catch. The next day, Fred and I were talking to Galen and mentioned how his son made a spectacular catch the night before. Galen had a somewhat disapproving look on his face, and gruffly replied, "If he ever does that again, I'll kick his ass."

Apparently, Grump was not impressed or amused.

Another time, we were playing the Angels in Anaheim in mid-September, and Ohio State was playing Oklahoma on ABC. During batting practice, they were showing the football game on the video board. The score was tied in the last seconds of the game, and Oklahoma kicked a field goal for the win. Galen, obviously ticked at the happenings on the video board, took off his cap, threw it from one end of the dugout to the other, and then turned and went back to the clubhouse. The dugout was extremely long, and we thought it was impossible to throw something that light that far. Evidently not when Ohio State loses.

Charley Lau, Hitting Coach

Charley Lau's two brightest and best pupils were George Brett and Hal McRae. He broke George down to the very basics. George was hitting about .185 at the time, and Charley helped turn him into a Hall of Fame hitter.

"I hit a whopping .125 when I came up in 1973. The next year at the All-Star break, with 200 at-bats, I was hitting .200 on the nose. Charley Lau told me that he thought I had a chance to play and a chance to hit, but he said, 'Obviously it's not working your way.' I think the approach he took with me was right on because he let me get to rock bottom. When you hit rock bottom and somebody wants to change some things, it's easier to accept

Charley Lau (left) and Lou Piniella always had engaging conversations on the art of hitting. *Photo courtesy of the Kansas City Royals*

it. ... Charley did a complete overhaul. He didn't make just one suggestion. He said, 'George, you've got to trust me on this. Give me your heart and give me your soul, and I can make you a player.' I gave him my heart and my soul. He changed my stance completely, he changed my philosophy and theory on hitting completely."

—George Brett

Ironically, Charley, a big-league catcher, was not a very good hitter, but really studied the art of hitting. He was a student of the game. As a teacher, however, he was good mentally and mechanically. He was very quiet, which meant that the hitter really had to listen closely to hear Charley. He was terrific. He taught me that most left-handed hitters were better low-ball hitters.

I have heard that Charley would call pitches from the dugout. George would look into the dugout, and Charley would signal to him what pitch was coming. He wasn't stealing signs; he just knew the game and the matchup between pitcher and hitter. He was a terrific teacher, and he was constantly studying ways to help players improve.

"Charley Lau was the best hitting coach ever in the game. One of my most intriguing and amusing after-game dinners was one night with Lau, Lou Piniella, and McRae. Charley stood up with a napkin, in the middle of the restaurant, and demonstrated his approach to a swing. Then Piniella stood up with a knife and fork and demonstrated his swing. I can hardly imagine what people thought."

—Buddy Blattner

Gene Mauch, Bench Coach

After a successful career as a manager, Gene Mauch came to the Royals as Bob Boone's bench coach. I loved talking to Gene, who, by the way, was a great golfer, about strategy and various big-league players, especially the major league players of the 1960s and '70s.

When I was growing up, I collected baseball cards. So often, before a game, Gene and I would sit on the bench during batting practice, I would think back to guys I didn't know much about from my baseball card collection, and ask him about them. He would give me a little two- or three-minute analysis of the player. He was making my old baseball cards come alive. It really was fascinating.

Chapter

5

ROYALS
HALL OF FAME PLAYERS

The highest organization-wide honor for someone involved with the Royals is induction into the team's Hall of Fame, which was established with the first class—Amos Otis and Steve Busby—in 1986.

After learning of my induction in 2003, I now can say that it is indeed humbling and quite a thrill to be selected for the team's Hall of Fame. I was taken aback when I learned of my induction for the 2004 season. Wow!

Three of the current Hall of Famers deservingly had their numbers retired: Dick Howser, former manager whose No. 10 was the first to be retired, in 1987; George Brett, whose No. 5 was retired on May 14, 1994; and Frank White, whose No. 20 was retired in 1995. The numbers and names of each man are displayed at the bottom of the Kauffman Stadium scoreboard.

In addition to the players about whom you will read on the following pages, four other people are in the team's Hall of Fame: Howser (1987), former general manager and president Joe Burke (1992), Ewing Kauffman (1993), and Muriel Kauffman (1996).

No. 5 George Brett

The thing I have said most often about George Brett is that he was the toughest player mentally that I have ever known or seen. That's why, to a large degree, he was so good in the clutch. He loved clutch situations. He loved being the guy who made everybody else more productive and better, because there wasn't as much pressure on them.

"I watched George grow from a pup of a player to a Hall of Famer. I consider myself fortunate to have seen a person play the game as well as he played it and to come through with so many clutch performances offensively and defensively, and to play the game with such unbounded joy. He was reflected as the Royals throughout the world."

—*John Schuerholz*

Coming up through the system, George was just another player in the minor leagues. He wasn't any type of "Can't-miss" prospect. However, he undoubtedly was mentally tough. Being the youngest of four boys, with the three in front of him very good athletes, he was under pressure to reach the level that they reached, which was pretty darn good.

The most well known Brett brother after George was Ken. Many people say he could have been as good a hitter as George if he hadn't been a pitcher. He was a great athlete. George may tell you that Ken was a better athlete.

Besides three older, successful brothers, George had the pressure of a demanding father. His father, who took no excuses, wanted his boys to succeed. So he pushed them to achieve.

With that background, George worked his way up through the organization.

The Master

The story of George's special relationship with hitting coach Charley Lau is well documented. After a few weeks in his first full year, George was hitting about .150. Charley asked him one day in Baltimore, "George, are you tired of hitting .150?" Of course, George said he was.

"Well, when we get back home, I'll meet you at the ballpark at two p.m. and we'll go to work."

From that point on, through Charley's incredible wisdom and George's unrelenting work ethic, George became a great hitter. He wasn't born that way. People just don't see all of the hard work he did, getting out to the stadium at 2:00 in the afternoon in the middle of the summer, when the temperature on that artificial turf was about 290 degrees, and working his hands to the bone with repetition after repetition.

Two young baseball fans take a trip through the past at the Kansas City Royals Hall of Fame. *Photo courtesy of the Kansas City Royals*

"George was on the bench with 1,999 hits and asked me if I had a bat that he could use. I did, but actually it was a bat that I stole out of Frank White's locker. George got a hit up the middle, number 2,000, and broke the bat. If you look at the video, you'll see the dark bat which George never used. When I was going up the runway after the game, I saw the bat in the trash can, so I took it up to him and he signed it for me."

—*Greg Pryor*

Then George had to work on his defense, particularly his throwing, which wasn't very good. His footwork wasn't all that great, but he worked his butt off and became a very good third baseman.

George never was a fast starter. By his birthday, though, which is May 15, when the weather would start to warm up, he was ready to go. Then, once he got into a groove and was in a real hot streak, man, he was sizzling. He had some unbelievable streaks throughout his career.

"We were sitting around in Cleveland after a game one time, having some beers, and we didn't have a ride back to the hotel. There was one of

those Pushman golf carts right outside the clubhouse, with some beer kegs on it. We decided we would take that back to the hotel. So we drove through the streets of Cleveland on that golf cart, hauling beer kegs. I think we might have lost a keg on the way back. We pulled into the hotel and had one of the bellmen drive the cart back."

—John Wathan

3,000, by George

As George was nearing 3,000 hits toward the end of the 1992 season, we were in California for a series with the Angels. George had 2,996 hits. Because of a shoulder injury, it was unknown whether he would play. The injury and George's pursuit of 3,000 combined were of concern because we were coming down to the end of the year, and he wanted to get it done that year because anything could happen injury-wise during the off-season. If he fell off his skis, or hit his head playing hockey, he might jeopardize his baseball career.

He went out there that night, with the pressure, and got the four hits that he needed. A couple of the hits were hard; a couple were seeing-eye hits. After the fourth hit, George got picked off first base, which gave some comic relief to the whole night.

It was neat that he got it done in California—where he grew up—in front of many of his family and friends. It would have been nice had George gotten it in Kansas City, but he didn't want to sit out of the games in California to wait for a return to K.C.

It was one of those nights where once the game started, and once he decided he was going to play, he was determined to get it done. He probably didn't think he'd get all four hits that night, but that's how it turned out.

Was that Bobby Orr?

During each winter, a group of us go out and play hockey regularly. Knowing we played, George asked, "Would you mind if I come out and play with you guys?" I was scared to death that he'd do something that would end his career. But he came out and loved it. Even though he hadn't skated much in his life—not many chances in Southern California in the 1960s—he had a blast. He picked up skating quickly.

He had so much fun that he dragged Jamie Quirk out there. Joe Zdeb came out one time.

The only problem was that he didn't know how to stop. The only way he could stop was to slam into the boards. That's not a real good idea.

One morning he said, "I'll race you for five bucks."

I said, "George, you've not skated very much. I've been skating since I was 16 years old."

That was his way of competing and trying to get better.

George also was fascinated by hockey fights. So he wanted to simulate a fight to see what it was like. I got him up against the boards and showed him how to pull his opponent's jersey over the guy's head so that his arms are pinned. When we were up against the boards, I was able to get his jersey over his head, get him down on the ice, and then get his bare back on the ice. He was kicking his feet, screaming "It's cold! It's cold! It's cold! Let me up!"

> *"We were all kind of horsing around when Denny and I squared off into a fake fight. Within 30 seconds, Denny had pulled my long-sleeved baseball undershirt over my head, like those bad fighters in the NHL. My arms were trapped and useless. The next thing I knew, my bare back was on the ice. After skating around for an hour, we were sweating, which made the ice even colder. It was pretty embarrassing to have the baseball radio announcer kick my butt on the ice!"*
>
> *—George Brett*

Bobby Orr, I was not. Wayne Gretzky, George was not. But we really did have a lot of fun!

The End of the Road

George was a great player to have on those Royals teams of the 1970s, '80s and early '90s. He helped set the tone for the hard-nosed play that many of the guys displayed. He often said during his career that on his last at-bat, "I want to hit a routine ground ball to second and bust it to first." That's how he played. Sure enough, that's nearly how he ended his career.

His last game was in Arlington against the Texas Rangers. It also was Nolan Ryan's final series. I remember when George came up for the last time, the Rangers were standing on the top step of their dugout, and the Royals were standing on the top step of their dugout, as a tribute. George hit a grounder through the middle that turned out to be a base hit. That was his last at-bat.

No. 20 Frank White

If ever a case could be made for Ewing Kauffman's school of innovative thinking, i.e. the Royals Baseball Academy, Frank White would be it. Frank, who grew up in Kansas City, went to Lincoln High School, which, ironically, was next to old Municipal Stadium. At the time, Lincoln didn't have a baseball team. He played during the summers, played in Kansas City's famed Ban Johnson League when he got older, but that's not quite the same as being able to start playing in March as high school teams do.

To many baseball people, Ewing's theory of "why can't we take a good athlete and make him a baseball player" didn't seem like a good idea. A player like Frank proved that it could work. Sure, Frank had played baseball, so the God-given talent already was there. They basically polished those skills, and then he further polished them in the minor leagues.

But just think what would have happened to Frank White had it not been for the Academy. In fact, he was married and working in a steel mill when he tried out for the Academy. So, without Ewing's idea, chances are, we never would have heard of Frank White.

Replacing a Favorite

Whitey Herzog was the one who placed Frank at second base permanently. Originally, Freddie Patek got hurt, so Frank came up from the minor leagues to play shortstop. Cookie Rojas, who was very popular with the fans, was still at second base.

When Whitey replaced Cookie with Frank, it wasn't very popular with the fans, but it was a move that needed to be made. (Think about this for a minute: Fans were upset when the hometown Frank White replaced Cookie Rojas at second.) Whitey was criticized for the move, and fans were on Frank a little bit at the start.

Cookie's range by that time had diminished to the point where he still had the great, sure hands, but couldn't get to as many balls, particularly on Astroturf. Frank was so quick and smooth that he could be standing in front of a grounder that Cookie would have trouble reaching.

"I didn't take as much criticism as Frank did when he took over second base in Kansas City, replacing fan favorite Cookie Rojas. ... Before that game [a game in Minnesota when Frank was starting] Cookie came into my office and said, 'Skipper, can you tell me why I'm not playing tonight?'

"I said, 'Cookie, we're back on Astroturf; Minnesota's got seven left-handed hitters in their lineup, and Frank goes 10 feet farther to his right and left, 100 feet farther back, and he comes in faster than you. Any other questions?'

"'No, that's all I wanted to know.' And he walked out.

"There are four things you want a second baseman to do: go left, go right, come in, and go out. Frank could do those four things better than any second baseman I have ever seen."

—Whitey Herzog

Wanting a strong defensive team, Whitey installed Frank at second base. Frank went on to become one of the greatest defensive second basemen ever to play the game. With Frank at second base, the team was much stronger up the middle.

Frank White and Jackie Robinson

Oddly enough, the one moment or game from Frank's career that I remember best is the great offensive game he had in St. Louis during the World Series.

Frank worked hard offensively, applied himself, and became better and better each year. He became so good offensively that during the 1985 World Series, he batted cleanup. In fact, he was only the second second baseman in the history of the game to hit cleanup in the World Series. (The other was Jackie Robinson.)

In the third game of that series, with the Royals down two games to none, Frank blasted a two-run homer in the fifth inning. He also had an RBI double, as the Royals won 6-1. Overall in the series, Frank led all Royals with six RBIs, and he had three doubles.

Frank became a really good clutch hitter. And because of the higher-profile offensive guys that we had, Frank probably did not get full credit for that. Everybody said that only George Brett was going to drive in the tough runs, which he did. Or if George doesn't, Hal McRae will drive in the tough runs, which he did. Frank drove in tough runs but didn't necessarily get the headlines that Mac and Brett got.

In fact, many may have forgotten that Frank was the Most Valuable Player of the 1980 American League Championship Series against the Yankees. Frank hit .545 in that series and had three RBIs, including a solo homer that gave the Royals the 1-0 lead in the decisive third game.

All of that underlines how far he came offensively and how hard he worked on all phases of his game. By the end of his career, Frank was really good offensively, and, of course, his defense speaks for itself.

Mr. Smooth

Defensively, Frank was automatic at second. He made so many outstanding plays, and made the outstanding plays look easy, that one does not surface above the others.

"There are two plays from Frank's career that come to mind immediately for me. In the 1977 American League playoffs against the Yankees, late in the game with the Royals leading, Frank made a diving, backhanded play on Reggie Jackson and flipped the ball to second base for the forceout. It was a play where I thought to myself how the Royals were going to win, especially when a guy is making that spectacular of a play. Unfortunately, they didn't win.

"The other play also happened during the 1980 playoffs in Yankee Stadium. A ball was grounded up the middle, and Frank crossed second base to make the play from the third base side of second and got the out at first. I looked back at Frank when the play was over, and he was standing where the shortstop was normally playing. I asked him after the game, 'Are you ever

surprised at where you are when a play is over?' He said, 'Today I was.' He just had incredible range."

—Fred White

Frank was smooth defensively. He wasn't an acrobatic player such as Ozzie Smith. Ozzie brought all the condiments with him. He had all the mustard and ketchup and pickles and everything else, so he would make a great play look spectacular. Frank didn't have all the condiments with him; he just made the good plays and great plays and made them look very routine.

The thing I remember about Frank is his ability to catch line drives. He had excellent leaping ability and an extraordinary ability to time his leap to catch the line drive. Those two components made him as good as anybody I've ever seen at any position.

His footwork around second base on double plays was superb. And those Royals teams in the 1970s might have aided in Frank taking some extra abuse. With guys such as George Brett, Hal McRae and others charging hard into second, many teams reciprocated that on Frank.

He had an incredible ability to get rid of the ball when a runner was bearing down on him. Fred White often describes Frank as being quick and light on his feet around second.

"I remember the first time I saw Frank play. He was called up as a shortstop in the middle of the 1973 season, which was also my first year with the Royals. We were on the road playing Baltimore. The first thing I thought about when I saw Frank around the bag at second was Bambi—he could move so quickly and jump so well. You could tell that it would be very difficult for incoming runners to get a hold of Frank on a double play."

—Fred White

The only time I remember Frank getting hurt at second base was in Boston. Dwight Evans slid in hard on Frank, who came down awkwardly and hurt his knee. That was the only time that Frank ever got really tangled up at second. Again, his footwork was so good that he could avoid guys barreling in at second.

"Frank White is the best second baseman I have ever seen play. He was like [dancer] Rudolf Nureyev at second base. Frank's athletic ability, agility, and physical play were unparalleled to me. In addition, he's a real classy guy."

           —John Schuerholz

Simply put, Frank was superb at second base.

Frank White, Welcome to Cooperstown

People will say that I'm prejudiced because of my appreciation for Frank and my thought that the Baseball Hall of Fame is too concerned with offensive stats, but if any player deserves to be in the Hall, it's Frank White.

The voters through the years, in my opinion, have not taken into account the importance of center fielders, second basemen, shortstops and catchers, the foremost important defensive positions. Maybe second base and shortstop are defensive positions that don't exactly translate to glamour for writers and broadcasters and fans.

But when you watch someone like Frank play every day for six or seven months, you begin to realize how important it is to have a solid second baseman defensively and a solid shortstop. You are not going to win many games if you don't. People want to talk about how many runs a guy produced as deserving of the Hall, but how many runs did your second baseman or shortstop prevent?

People want to say that Bill Mazeroski was the best second baseman ever. That's fine, because I didn't see him play. But I don't see how Maz, who now is in the Hall of Fame, could be much better than Frank.

"Frank White was the best defensive second baseman I have ever seen. I've seen second basemen that were pretty darn good, such as Bobby Richardson and Bill Mazeroski. Frank played second base for me for five years, and I just don't see how you play the position defensively any better than he played it."

           —Whitey Herzog

Frank should be a very solid nominee for the Hall of Fame. There are no questions about his credentials. Frank played second base for a long time as well as second base has ever been played. It will be a travesty if he never makes it.

However, if Frank never makes it to Cooperstown, in 2004 he received an honor that is almost as incredible, when the Royals placed a statue of Frank outside Kauffman Stadium, along the right-field line. Anytime a team puts a statue up for you, it's high praise. But Frank deserved it.

"I think the statue's off the charts; it's hard to compare it with anything, including the Baseball Hall of Fame. The Hall of Fame is an exciting time, but when you've had as much success as I've had in Kansas City and been honored in so many ways, the Hall of Fame is something I never think about. If I ever get there, it won't be for me—it'll be for the fans and others who think I deserve induction. So many things have happened for me that I don't see the Hall of Fame as a major step anymore. Winning the '85 World Series still is the ultimate, but the statue itself is kind of like a Hall of Fame to me. This is it. Most people aren't around when statues are made of them."

—Frank White

The funny thing about that to me is that a statue does him complete injustice because he was never frozen on the field. He did not resemble a statue when he played; he never stood still on the field. But it's certainly a well-earned distinction. Really cool.

The Thinking Man's Player

From the time I first met Frank in 1973, he's been quiet, but he's not afraid to share some interesting insights into things. When he was playing, since I had played second through college, I would always enjoy asking him questions regarding the nuances of second base. I learned a lot from him just by talking to him.

Frank always gave me great insights on second base play and the state of baseball. He wouldn't give just three- or four-word answers; he would elaborate on everything. So I enjoyed picking his brain. Frank is a very thoughtful person. He's cognizant of other people's feelings, and he's a thinker.

After spending a couple of years in the Royals' front office, in 2004 Frank started managing the Royals' Class AA team in Wichita. He undoubtedly has the ability to be a great manager.

CLASS OF 1986

Amos Otis

Centerfielder Amos Otis will always be one of the best outfielders to play for the Royals. He was a true five-tool player. He could do it all. For the Royals, he did. He won three Gold Glove Awards in center and batted .280 with 193 home runs and 992 RBIs.

Amos was the Royals' first major star, which he obviously wasn't with the Mets. He was just working his way into their ball club, but they badly needed a third baseman, so Cedric Tallis made the deal, sending Joe Foy to the Mets for Otis and Bob Johnson. Foy had a career year for the Royals in 1969, so Cedric was able to make the trade. Amos played third in the Mets' system until they moved him to the outfield.

Amos, who was the first Royals player to actually play in an All-Star Game, helped give us that all-important strength up the middle.

Center field was a great fit. Amos made things look very easy and fluid out there. You watch some guys run and it's obvious they're running hard to get to a ball. Amos didn't appear to be running hard, but he was going full tilt. That was just the mechanics of his body. Former Royal Carlos Beltran is the same way. The body mechanics of Beltran and Otis don't allow them to look like they're running hard.

Guys like Amos and Carlos are smooth, and they build up speed without you realizing it. But that's the only way they can run. You can't change the way you run; I don't care if you go out there in front of your house and practice running differently all day. You're basically going to run the same and look the same.

In addition to having a strong arm, Amos had really good judgment on his throws. He rarely made a bad throw. Some people may remember the All-Star Game when Pete Rose went barreling into catcher Ray Fosse. That throw, which was perfect, was from A.O. in center field.

Amos also was a good judge of fly balls and what it took to get to each one. I remember him hitting the fence only once. It was at

Municipal Stadium against the Orioles, on a Sunday afternoon in 1972 before the All-Star break.

Bobby Grich crushed the ball, and A.O. crashed into the wall. I don't remember if he hurt something on his arm or his shoulder, but he missed some time after that. From that point on, he seemed to be of the mindset, "I'm never going to run straight into a wall again." I don't think he ran into a wall hard from that point on.

"I had the darkest glasses in baseball that allowed me to look directly into the sun and find the ball. Baltimore's outfield wall was dark green. Usually I would turn, run, find the wall, flip down the glasses and find the ball. This time I turned to go back, flipped my glasses before finding the wall, and I couldn't tell where I was. I turned back around, saw the ball, and nailed the wall. They took me off behind the wall on a stretcher. The next batter, Boog Powell, hit a homer over the center field wall and it hit me on the stretcher. They took me to the hospital, and I was there until Wednesday and also missed the All-Star Game. Even after the break, when I came back I was a little gun-shy. That wall will make you humble."

—Amos Otis

That was kind of a turning point in his career as an outfielder. He still played aggressively and robbed hitters of home runs, but he knew where he was on the field, and he started playing about 10 feet deeper.

Even though Amos caught with two hands when he got here, he soon became comfortable using one. That became his trademark over the years.

"I had a teammate in 1970 with the Royals named Pat Kelly, who had trouble catching fly balls. He had both hands in the air waiting for the ball. I told him how all sorts of things can happen when both hands are in the air too long. To show him what I was talking about, I wouldn't raise my throwing hand to catch the ball. Catching with one hand started to feel so good that it was natural. Pat ended up catching everything one-handed. Obviously, I stayed with it. I had a rhythm that allowed me to get rid of the ball on my throws a lot quicker after I caught it."

—Amos Otis

The Glove

Amos used a big, big glove that his brother had given him while he was growing up in Alabama. Looking at that glove, it's easy to see why he could catch so easily with one hand. Another interesting aspect of that glove is that it had a hole in the palm.

"The hole was there because I used to put so much pine tar and Stickum inside the glove. Almost the whole inside of my glove was covered with Stickum. Eventually, the middle of it started cracking and peeling, so I cut a little bit off. The next thing I knew, I cut a hole big enough to put a softball through. It also came in handy when rowdy fans in a place like New York would get on me. Instead of making an obvious obscene gesture and getting fined, I could stick my fist through that hole and let them know what I thought."

—Amos Otis

If I remember correctly, that glove also was stolen once or twice.

"It was stolen three times. Joe Garagiola showed the glove on television one night, showing people how big the hole was, and that I could slip my hand and arm all the way through it and set it on my shoulder. A little bit after that, it was stolen in Kansas City. I went on TV and said how I wanted it back because it was special. I said that if the person would send it back, with no questions asked I would send them two new gloves, a bat and a ball. The glove showed up. I sent the two new gloves, a bat and a ball, with no questions asked.

"Then someone broke into the clubhouse in Milwaukee and stole our stuff. I happened to walk by the trash can in the trainer's room, and my glove was in there, probably because it had that big hole. Then in Ft. Myers, somebody stole our stuff. I checked in the trash can, and there was my glove. The same person or people stole it twice, I think."

—Amos Otis

The Home Run

Defense wasn't the only strong part of Amos Otis's game. He was a threat at the plate and on the basepaths. Amos Otis hit one of the longest home runs ever at Royals Stadium in a night game against Rollie Fingers and Milwaukee. He hit it up around the top of the flagpole in left field. Had it not hit the flagpole, it might have left the stadium, which no player has done. It was in the ninth inning, and I want to say that it was early in the season on a night that you wouldn't expect the ball to carry that much.

"They tell me that there's a question mark next to who hit the longest home run at Royals Stadium. Some say it was Bo Jackson. There's no question with me—if my ball hadn't hit the flagpole, I think it would have left the stadium. I've attended a couple functions where Rollie Fingers was speaking, and he'll tell the audience that the person who hit the longest homer off him is in the audience, but that I was using a corked bat.

"You bet it was corked—from the top to the bottom. I didn't use one often, but I sometimes brought it out late in the game. A corked bat should be a weapon that you use late in the game when your team needs an extra run or some excitement. That's what I was doing that night."

—Amos Otis

Before you start talking about his home runs and a corked bat, understand that it's been said that a corked bat really doesn't add that much distance to a home run. It adds some, but it doesn't explain Amos Otis's power. Holy smokes, he had surprising power. He didn't look like he would because he wasn't that prototypical power guy in build, but he had some pop in him. Boy, he was very wiry but strong.

Also offensively, Amos was a great base stealer. He had 340 stolen bases for the Royals in 410 chances. That's an incredible percentage. You had the feeling that Amos could steal a base any time he wanted to.

"I would probably have to say that I took the most pride in my base stealing. I made bets with my teammates, such as U.L. Washington. I would tell them that I could steal second base standing up against a certain pitcher. We'd bet a dinner with all the trimmings in the next town we visited. Then

I'd steal a base and would wipe the dust off my shoes. I usually could do that when I wanted to."

—*Amos Otis*

By the way, Frank White remembers Amos doing that.

That's Just A.O.

Amos Otis and I got along great, which not everyone in the media can claim. I was one of the few guys to whom he would talk. I got some good material from Amos because we got along well. I called him A.O. and he called me Denver. (I think John Mayberry called me Denver, too.) Amos would bug me about a pregame show, saying, "Denver, when are we going to do a pregame show? Are you going to have me on again?" I'd jokingly say, "Nah, A.O., I don't want you on any more. I'm tired of talking to you." We had fun with that.

He was always a good interview when he set his mind to it. He always had some interesting things to say, and he had an interesting personality. I don't think he really wanted a lot of people to get to know him. He could be defensive with his personality, but I always liked him very much. We got along great after our first interview in 1970.

"Amos Otis got an earful from me one time. We would do interviews early so we could have them for the pregame show. This particular day, Denny, who was a young broadcaster at the time, was trying to get Amos for an interview. Amos kept putting him off. He kept delaying and delaying until it was too late. Finally, with a few minutes to spare, Denny went back up to the booth and told me he couldn't get Amos. So I told him to just interview me and we'd go from there.

"I saw Amos later, and I told him that I didn't appreciate what he did to Denny and that he would never be on the pregame or postgame show until he apologized. Even if that was Amos's personality, he shouldn't have treated Denny that way. Several games later, Amos came up and apologized. We had him on the show that night, and he was great from that point on."

—*Buddy Blattner*

That was just Amos. He had a mystique. I think he was very guarded. I wouldn't say that he was a loner, but I think he was fine by himself and he just liked to have fun with the media. Instead of throwing a tirade as some players and coaches do, A.O. would be sarcastic or simply not talk.

Amos had a great wit. He always impressed me as being really bright, brighter than he wanted people to know. His light was bright, but he had it on dim just so people wouldn't get too close.

Just How Far Are We Going, Denver?

The team went from Ft. Myers to Jacksonville, Florida, to play an exhibition game. We were in the hotel at Jacksonville, and nobody knew much about the city (which, by the way, is where I was born, but I only spent six weeks there). We particularly didn't know where to eat. My room was on the 23rd floor of this hotel, so I could see easily down this long, busy street that ran in front of the hotel.

Even though it was getting dark, with my binoculars I spotted a McDonald's down the street. So I wandered down into the lobby ready to run down to the golden arches. Amos was in the lobby, and we started chitting and chatting. We mentioned how hungry we were, so I said, "From my room, I saw McDonald's just down the street; we could walk down there and get a burger if you want."

"Ah, that sounds good to me," Amos replied. "I don't want to get involved with a big deal with dinner tonight." And we started walking.

Well, damn my binoculars ... from the 23rd floor of the hotel, that McDonald's must have been three miles down the road. Over the last two and a half miles, Amos was bitching every step of the way.

"Where is this place, Ft. Myers?" he said, among other things, a few times.

We finally got there and ate our burgers, but yes, it felt as if we'd walked to Ft. Myers. By the time we completed the walk back to the hotel, which, of course, included more bitching from A.O., we were hungry again.

Steve Busby

I remember seeing Steve Busby pitch batting practice at Anaheim Stadium right after he signed with the Royals out of the University of

Southern California. The guys watching him throw BP were saying, "Oooo, that's pretty nasty stuff."

Buzz was school smart, street smart and pitching smart. In today's game, I think a nice comparison is with the Cubs' Mark Prior, who also came out of USC.

Buzz had a great slider, great fastball, and he was ultra-competitive. You obviously have to have that drive to make it to the major leagues, but there are different competitive levels in the big leagues. Buzz would have been right at the top of ultra-competitive, almost to the point where he would fight himself a little bit. That is the other side of being so competitive. But 95 percent of the time he channeled it productively.

Fore! Or Rather, Make that Three!

Buzz is easy to get along with, has a good sense of humor, is a great golfer, and is fun to play golf with. When I first started to play golf, Busby and I would play together once in a while at spring training. He could hit the ball a mile. He hit it high and far. He was the only guy I ever played golf with or have seen play golf who could have three balls in the air at the same time.

He'd hit one a mile high and mile far, but he wouldn't like it, so he'd tee up another and whack it, cuss at himself because he didn't like it, and go through the process again. Talk about rapid load and rapid fire; that was Buzz playing golf.

No-No Times Two

Busby's two no-hitters would be the things that would come to my mind first of all when I think about his career. The first no-hitter was against the Tigers and a good Detroit team with solid hitters. The second one was in Milwaukee.

The one in Detroit was early in the year, on a real windy, cool night. At that time in baseball, pitch counts were not that big a deal, and I know Buzz threw a lot of pitches.

"I knew what was going on, but it wasn't until the ninth inning that a no-hitter started to creep into the forefront of my mind. Then I just had fun. It seemed like everything happened so fast in the ninth inning, and yet I threw a whole bunch of pitches.

"That was a Detroit team that was just a couple years removed from the World Series. They had a lot of veteran players, but it was a very cold night. They didn't want to hit. It was a miserable night in their old stadium, and they just wanted to get the game over with and get out of there. I was more than happy to oblige the best I could."

—*Steve Busby*

Then for the one in Milwaukee, second baseman Cookie Rojas made a great play late in the game that saved the no-hitter. We had a better than normal view of that play because we weren't in our normal broadcast spot. We were broadcasting the game from the right field corner because they were renovating the press box at County Stadium. Imagine calling pitches from the right field corner; that was a treat.

"In the eighth inning, I helped save the no-hitter by diving for a ball to my left that was going to be a base hit. It was great to be a part of that game. Busby was one of the best pitchers I ever saw in my life. He proved how good he was while he was pitching. He had great stuff, great command. He's the one who started the third-to-first pickoff move. He was very successful at doing that."

—*Cookie Rojas*

When Busby got that second no-hitter, we all wondered how many no-hitters he would throw in his career. He was just dominant.

Unfortunately, he injured his rotator cuff, and he wasn't the same after that. I remember when he got hurt. We were in Anaheim, in the 12th inning, and he was still pitching. I can only imagine how many pitches he threw, but pitch count wasn't a big deal back then. He wanted to stay in the game, and manager Jack McKeon obliged.

Buzz was the first pitcher to have rotator cuff surgery and make a comeback. He missed all of the 1977 season and part of '78, and then pitched all of 1980 and part of '81.

The Makeup of a Hall of Famer

Many will say that had Buzz not gotten injured, he could have been one of the game's best pitchers ever. He was comparable to Tom Seaver.

Again, as with so many things in this game, we'll never know how good Busby would have been.

Buzz pitched with Don Drysdale's mentality. He pitched inside; he wasn't afraid to hit a guy with a pitch. He'd drill you, given the slightest provocation. One game he had buzzed a guy twice, and I asked him later that night, "Were you trying to move him off the plate?"

Very matter-of-factly, Buzz said, "No, I was trying to hit him in the neck." He went on to tell me why, but I don't remember now.

That's the way he pitched. He threw with that old-school mentality.

The Grand Slam That Wasn't

Steve Busby was a very good hitter. We were playing in Anaheim, and the Royals were in the first base dugout. Busby was at the plate with the bases loaded. The umpire at first had called a strike on a check swing, and the guys in the dugout were all over him. Paul Splittorff was at the end of the dugout near first base.

Busby, who was a big, strong guy, got a hold of one and jolted it. It looked like one of his golf drives, high and deep. Way out of the ballpark for a grand slam homer. The Royals' dugout was going goofy. All of a sudden, we looked down and the first base umpire had his hands up in the air. He had called time, and he kicked Splittorff out of the game (he wasn't pitching, but he was ejected) for something he said.

Buzz and Split were roommates on the road, and they got along great. Split told me, "For years and years I never told Buzz that I was the guy that got his grand slam home run negated."

CLASS OF 1987

Paul Splittorff

Paul Splittorff was the first ever signed by the Royals in the minor leagues. And he was the first person to pitch for the organization. He went to the minor leagues and pitched for the Royals before the big club even had a team. He also was the Royals' starting pitcher in April 1973, in the first game at Royals Stadium.

He comes off as serious, but Splittorff was always in the middle of everything, stirring things up and enjoying the banter. He was careful to listen and then throw in his two cents. I think that is probably the thing he missed the most when he retired as a player. He was deliberate like that on the mound, also.

Split was one of those guys who got the maximum out of his physical abilities. He worked hard, was competitive and paid attention to detail. He didn't have an eye-popping fastball or a knee-buckling curve or a wonderful change-up. He had good stuff, but he used intelligence and competitiveness game after game after game.

Not everybody has a Nolan Ryan fastball with good movement, or a Sandy Koufax curveball. Those are rare. So the other good pitchers are guys who have known how to pitch. They have adjusted during a game or during an inning or during a hitter. Pitchers have to think their way through the game; the pitcher has to be smarter than the hitter. Split would very much fall into that category.

He's applied that same mentality to his work now as a broadcaster. He's worked hard at it, and he's become a good one in both baseball and basketball.

Cookie Rojas

Cookie Rojas came to the Royals from the Cardinals in 1970 in a trade for Fred Rico, the outfielder who also was the team barber. Cookie brought the element of experience, class, and big-league smarts to the team. That really helped the expansion team at the time. He replaced Jerry Adair at second base.

Cookie's hands were superb. He rarely fumbled a ball and rarely made a bad or a dumb play.

Cookie was very serious but with a good sense of humor underneath, where you'd have to pull it out of him. He always had interesting things to say. He really studied the game, and he really worked at the game.

The Homer That Almost Wasn't

As a member of the Royals, Cookie hit a home run in the 1972 All-Star Game in Atlanta. So he had some pop in his bat. Representing the Royals in '72, he was the ninth player to go to the All-Star Game for both the American and National League. The problem with that home run in '72, though, is that Cookie almost didn't get a chance to hit it.

"By the seventh inning, Rod Carew was still playing second. I went over to have a drink of water next to [manager Earl Weaver] and he said, 'Do you mind if I don't use you?' I said, 'Wait a minute, Weaver. Anyone who is selected for a team of All-Stars selected by the fans should participate. As a matter of fact, Rod Carew has a pulled muscle in his right side. I don't know if you knew that.' He didn't, so he went down to the other end of the bench and asked Carew. Rod said, 'I had been hurting for a few days before I even got to the All-Star Game.' Earl came back and told me that if Carlton Fisk, who was on deck, got on base, then I would pinch hit. We were losing 2-1 at the time.

"When they announced at Atlanta Stadium that Cookie Rojas was batting for Rod Carew, I got booed because I was hitting for the best hitter in baseball. With Fisk on base, I hit a home run that put us ahead. Earl Weaver was at the top of the dugout steps, happy as heck, when I got back, and he stretched his arms out to me. I basically told him to put his hands where the sun doesn't shine. I couldn't believe it; one second he wasn't going to use me and now he wanted to shake my hand."

—Cookie Rojas

The Club's First Double-Play Combo

Cookie Rojas and Freddie Patek were the team's first long-term double-play combination. And they were a good one. They were the first guys I ever saw work the play where, on a ground ball up the middle, the second baseman gets to it, backhands it and flips it to the shortstop with a backhand motion of the glove.

The first time I remember them doing it was in Boston in front of a packed Fenway Park crowd. The Red Sox fans gave Cookie and Freddie a great ovation for that play.

The Cuban Connection

Cookie was born and raised in Cuba. He still had relatives there when he was with us in the 1970s, so he was very, very concerned with the political situation in Cuba with Castro being the dictator. He would talk about that from time to time, and you could tell that it was toward the forefront of his mind constantly.

Today

Cookie was a very popular Royal, as I mentioned in Frank White's story. The fans here really took to him. It likely was a combination of his nickname, his demeanor, and the way he played.

One of Cookie's sons, Victor, who pretty much grew up in the Kansas City area, now is a major league broadcaster. His first season with the Arizona Diamondbacks was 2003. Cookie spent the 2003 season enjoying life in Miami.

CLASS OF 1989

Dennis Leonard

Dennis Leonard was a workhorse. In his own way, he probably was as competitive as Busby, but not as outwardly so. Leo was a Hoover when it came to sucking up innings and complete games. He still holds the club record for career complete games (103) and career shutouts (23).

Away from the field, he was a man's man. He and manager Whitey Herzog would go fishing early in the mornings. Leo loves to fish and hunt. Somebody once said that Leo reminds them of Yosemite Sam, the cartoon character. That's a pretty good description.

He's just a cool guy with a nice family. You always feel good being around Leo. We were on the Royals' caravan together in the winter before the 2003 season. It was a blast to hear him recount things and retell some incredible stories.

April 12, 1986

One of my favorite games as a broadcaster was Leonard's comeback game against Toronto after blowing out his knee. It was such an incredible story, because three years prior, on May 28, 1983, facing Baltimore's Cal Ripken Jr., Leo severed his patella tendon.

Over the next three years, Leo went through multiple and painful surgeries and rehab. Once he was ready to come back, he was going to be worked slowly into the rotation. Instead, on the last day of spring training in 1986, Danny Jackson twisted his ankle on a sprinkler head in the outfield while running. So here comes Leo, earlier than planned, starting for the world champion Royals. You couldn't tell that he had missed any time.

> *"All of a sudden, I'm starting a game at home on national TV. I didn't want to embarrass myself. I wanted to go five good innings and do the best I could.*
>
> *"If I had any bit of nervousness, it was not to be embarrassed. As the game progressed, I figured that if I got knocked out in the fourth inning, I did pretty well. Everything worked out. It was a storybook ending to three years of misery.*
>
> *"It's kind of weird, but that was my World Series. I never worked that hard between starts in my life, from that game in 1983 to my next start in 1986! If I had any guts, I would've quit after that Toronto game. I told myself that it wouldn't get any better than that.*
>
> *"I want to thank the Kansas City fans. There were about 26,000 people there that day against Toronto. They treated me like I won the seventh game of the World Series."*
>
> —Dennis Leonard

That was a cold Saturday afternoon. Watching Leonard pitch that day, gutting his way through that game and really pitching a beautiful game, it was one of those broadcasts where everything just flowed.

He threw an incredible game that April day. He allowed just three hits and went the distance. One of the hits came with two outs in the ninth inning. Leo struck out the game's final batter, former Royal Rance Mulliniks. The Royals won 1-0.

I watched Audrey, Leo's wife, and the two kids sitting behind home plate, and I was doing almost as much play-by-play on their reaction as as I was to the action on the field. It was cool watching them. Audrey used to get so wrapped up to the games anyway, and that day was even more special.

That is one of my favorite games in Royals history.

Leo and the Bird

The other game that comes to mind when I think of Leo is the game that he pitched against Mark "Bird" Fidrych in Detroit in 1976.

Talk about a perfect night for baseball. That old ballpark was packed, because Fidrych was the hot item, plus it was a perfect night, weather-wise. Leonard and the Royals won that game 1-0.

That was another of those dream games for a broadcaster.

"In 1976, we had four position players make the All-Star team, which was common back then. Shortly before the All-Star break, we were playing in New York and then Detroit. Whitey [Herzog] told me that he was going to hold me back because I made the All-Star team. In that particular year, Al Fitzmorris had a great record, Paul Splittorff had a great record, Doug Bird was starting, and he had a great record. I was 9-2 at that point.

"I grew up in New York, and I remember telling my dad that I wasn't going to be pitching there because I made the All-Star team. ... Well, P.S., Whitey apologized to me, saying that he didn't know what happened, but I didn't make the All-Star team. So, I went from being a big, tall stud, to becoming a little, itty-bitty nothing.

"My father-in-law, God bless him, flew to Detroit to meet us. We were in a little piano bar, I was drinking water, and I told him, 'Fidrych my [butt], I'm going to beat him tomorrow.'

"During the game, we had a runner on third, and Hal McRae hit a grounder to deep second base to score a run. ... It was one of those situations where we were determined to win."

—*Dennis Leonard*

Hal McRae

I've enjoyed talking hitting with Hal McRae as much as any player I've been around in the game. He can really get into the mechanics, the whys and the wherefores, and the mindset of the pitcher and hitter. It's always compelling, really interesting stuff.

Mac always called me Den-eh. "Hey, Den-eh." (I think the "y" was in his heart, but it just wouldn't come out.) Mac always would have a little libation after every game. That was one of his habits. You knew that he wouldn't run around at night, but he would go into the hotel lounge and have a cold beer after a game. Anybody who would want to come in and sit down and chat, Mac would sit there and chat with you until you were done chatting. I wish I had had a tape recorder all of the times that I just sat in the lounge and had a beer with Mac and talked hitting.

The other side of Mac was his sense of humor. It's as good as anybody's sense of humor that I've ever come across in baseball. He was funny and could tell stories. Plus, his laugh is infectious.

Mac the Knife

McRae was as hard-nosed and aggressive as any player that the Royals have ever had. He had a high intensity and competitiveness that he brought with him from Cincinnati. I think it was infectious, because George Brett caught it immediately. George was not immune to the Hal McRae disease that he brought over from Cincinnati. They ran the bases like a couple of men possessed. And everybody else kind of caught on to that style of play.

Nobody could forget the "McRae Rule," from one of the playoff series with the Yankees, when, breaking up a double play, McRae knocked second baseman Willie Randolph into left center field.

Desire to DH

During winter ball in Puerto Rico in 1968, while Mac was in the Reds' organization, he broke his leg in four places. He never ran nearly as well after that. They say that before that, he was an extremely fast runner. He wasn't the same after it.

But that didn't stop his determination and his desire to become a better hitter. Charley Lau's theories and teachings probably helped McRae as much as they helped Brett. Mac became baseball's first bona fide designated hitter. He was a good outfielder, but he will always be known as a great DH.

CLASS OF 1992

Fred Patek

Even though Freddie Patek was short in stature (five foot four), he had some good physical abilities. He was a good runner who everybody thought was a lot faster than he was. His legs, going at 100 miles per hour, made him look as if he were running faster. But he was a very good base stealer. In fact, he led the league in steals in 1977 with 53.

Defensively, Freddie, whom the Royals got from Pittsburgh, had an excellent arm and good range. He also was good offensively, especially when he was just trying to make contact.

Like middle infield mate Cookie Rojas, Freddie was popular with the fans in Kansas City. People identified with him because of his lack of size and because he overcame some odds. I'm sure a lot of scouts early in his career said, "He's never going to make the big leagues because he is not big enough." He was a good guy for the Royals from 1971-79 and always a great interview. In one of my favorite quotes, someone asked Freddie how it felt to be the smallest player in the major leagues. He replied, "It's better than being the smallest player in the minor leagues."

Larry Gura

Larry Gura was a thinking man's pitcher, and then some. He didn't have great stuff, but he was smart enough to put it all together and give Kansas City some terrific years with some great games. He was one of the best defensive pitchers we ever have had. He worked hard on the little things, such as the pickoff move to first, fielding bunts, etc. He sometimes asked me to come out early on Sunday mornings and bunt to him, so he could practice coming off the mound.

Larry was enjoyable to talk with because he dissected everything. I always thought of him as a very cerebral type. He analyzed everything and was the opposite of impulsive. The team always could count on a solid effort by Larry every time out.

CLASS OF 1996

John Mayberry

The Royals needed a big RBI/home run guy, and John Mayberry was the man. He came to the Royals in a trade with Houston. He ran into some problems in Houston with his hitting instructor, Harry Walker. Walker was the kind of instructor who wanted guys to make contact and hit the ball to the opposite field. John was not that type of hitter. He was a home run/RBI guy. He was up there to rip one.

When the Royals got big John, we were still playing at Municipal Stadium, and it had a fairly short porch in right field. He was perfect for that.

As you've probably already seen in this book, John was one of the great characters we had on the team. He's a great storyteller with a big, booming voice. He also had a knack for riding pretty much anyone on the team.

"Most of the time on the bus, Big John would get on people just to keep the guys loose. I remember one time when he was a little ticked, though. For three or four games straight, Big John would get knocked down or hit. Our pitchers didn't retaliate. I think we were in Milwaukee when Big John was fed up. He got on the bus and announced, 'The next time I get knocked down or hit, and they don't get knocked down, I'm going to kick your ass, your ass, your ass,' and he went down the line pointing at some of the pitchers. Even though Big John could needle you, most guys wouldn't want to get into it with him. In the next game, John got knocked down. Sure enough, it seems that most of the other team's batters got knocked down that night after that."

—*Amos Otis*

Diamond Jim

John had a nickname for everybody. His nickname for Orioles pitcher Jim Palmer was "Diamond Jim." We were in Baltimore for a series, and Palmer was going to pitch one game.

He bedeviled John with that big, slow, sloppy change-up every once in a while. He had gotten John out a couple of times in a previous game in Kansas City with that pitch.

During batting practice in Baltimore, John came out of the cage and announced, "Diamond is in trouble tonight. I'm going to wait on that change and then POW!"

In his second at-bat, John got the change-up. He waited and waited and waited. And then he took a murderous hack, and PHHHTTT! right off the end of the bat. He barely hit it one foot in front of home plate. John was horrified to see the ball just spinning like a top in front of home. He was not even going to run. I'd say Diamond got the best of Big John that time.

CLASS OF 1998

Dan Quisenberry

Dan Quisenberry was one of my all-time favorite people. He was a wordsmith, always intrigued by the English language. We would give each other a word of the day. He would have to work his into his postgame interview, and I would have to work the one he gave me into the broadcast. I gave him the word "gelid" one night in Detroit. (The word means extreme cold.) It just happened to be cold that night in Detroit. Quiz finished the game.

After the game, when the media was around his locker, Quiz said, "You never know what kind of stuff you will have when it is tough to grip the ball under such gelid conditions." You could tell many of the reporters didn't have a clue what the word meant.

Quiz's sense of humor was off the charts. Some of his quotes were hilarious. His sense of humor was unusual. I was completely intrigued by it. His vocabulary was superb. A conversation with the Quiz always was an adventure.

"Quiz was always so funny. Most of us can't tell jokes because we start laughing, but he did it with a straight face the whole time. You never could tell if he was being honest or just pulling your leg. One time, Charlie Leibrandt, Sabes [Bret Saberhagen], Quiz and I were hanging out at a bar in Boston called Daisy Buchannan's, and people started coming up and talking to us. Quiz started telling people that he was going to invent an underwater Nautilus machine that would make everyone bigger and stronger. A huge audience gathered around him, thinking he was telling the truth. Of course, he kept a straight face the whole time. He was talking about how he put a Nautilus machine underwater to add to the resistance. This group of people believed everything he said. Meanwhile, I was on the ground, dying of laughter, and people thought I was stupid because I was laughing at Quiz's 'invention.' He kept it going and going. By the end, I think if he would've had it, he would've sold out.

"The thing about Quiz is that when you saw him out of uniform, you would've bet everything you had that he wasn't an athlete. Not that he didn't

have an athletic body, but his vocabulary, the clothes he wore and the way he projected himself, you never would've thought he was hanging out in a clubhouse a couple hours before. He was an awesome human being."

—Mark Gubicza

Necessity Breeds a Winner

Out of necessity, Quiz was called up in 1978 to see what he could do with the club. He threw the submarine style, which meant he threw a lot of sinkers.

We had a good infield, and his sinkers resulted in a lot of ground balls, which was a good combination. He was confident, not to the point of cocky, but just confident that he could get hitters out. I think he had the perfect personality for a closer. He was a good person in every respect.

"Dan Quisenberry was very special. When he first came up and I caught him in the bullpen, I thought, why is this guy here? He was a side-armer who threw maybe 83 miles per hour. Who was he going to get out?

"We used to sit together in the bullpen. His routine in the bullpen was to do the crossword puzzle early in the game. All of us in the bullpen would try to guess the attendance at home games. So Quiz and I would sneak back into George Toma's office about the fifth inning and call to find out what the attendance was. We would 'guess' close enough that we won all the time. Nobody could figure out how we did that. Then he would start to get serious about the sixth inning, and be ready to pitch."

—John Wathan

Quiz's greatest ally as a pitcher was the ego of the hitter. Hitters were confident that they could hit him. And they often tried to do too much. One of the games I missed was against the Yankees in our ballpark. Reggie Jackson hit a line drive over the center field fence. That was one of the few home runs against Quiz. He usually kept the ball in play.

It's easy to see why he finished with 238 saves and a club-record 2.55 ERA during his career.

CLASS OF 2000

Willie Wilson

Willie Wilson was a great high school football player. He actually had a chance to play in college at Maryland. Luckily for Royals fans, he chose to sign with the Royals.

I met him the day he signed and chatted with him. He had the look of an exceptional athlete. He was tall and lean. He had the look of a runner.

With Willie's speed, the thing that turned his career around was learning to switch hit. He resisted that at first, but then he became very good at it. It is hard as a professional to start learning to switch hit, but Willie did. Whitey Herzog was a big factor in him figuring out what type of player Willie was or could be. The idea was to put the ball in play and then use your speed. It worked. In 1980, he became just the second player in baseball history to collect 100 hits from each side of the plate in the same season.

Willie was also a great base stealer and tremendous defensive player. The only drawback was that his arm was not that strong.

Willie was very headstrong and highly competitive, sometimes over the top. He's a proud person. He could be moody at times early in his career, but then maturity set in and it wasn't a problem.

Oh, What a Year!

Willie was an offensive force. In 1980, the same year he had 230 hits, he went to the plate 705 times. He was a tough out. If he hit a ball in the gap, look out! Watching him run out a triple or an inside-the-park home run was one of the most exciting things you could see.

Willie probably could have outrun anyone in baseball. Willie had both quickness and speed.

After facing some personal struggles in the 1990s, Willie seemingly has landed on his feet. During 2003, he managed an independent baseball team in Canada.

CLASS OF 2003

Jeff Montgomery

Jeff Montgomery came to the Royals from Cincinnati before the 1988 season for Van Snider. At the time, that wasn't a big trade. The Royals didn't have any idea where they were going to use Monty.

The number-one drawback to Monty in the eyes of a lot of scouts and other baseball people was his size. Now, if he had been a left-hander, his size wouldn't have been much of a factor. Have you ever noticed how size is always a factor with a right-handed pitcher but it isn't with a left-hander? For whatever reason, in the last 30-35 years, there haven't been many outstanding right-handed pitchers who were not six feet tall. Monty wasn't six feet tall.

Another drawback to Montgomery was that he never was a "can't-miss" prospect. And thirdly, he didn't really have a role; nobody knew if he was a starter, a long relief guy, or a closer. And his fourth drawback was that he didn't have a dominating pitch. Finally, when he came to us, Monty really didn't pitch with much rhythm and tempo.

Now, how in the hell did he get into the Royals Hall of Fame?

Monty was the club's only option as a closer in 1989. As it turned out, he fit into that role perfectly, both mentally and physically. He was competitive, a hard worker, and once he got rhythm and tempo, his control improved on all four pitches.

He wasn't the prototypical closer with one or two dominating pitches; he was a closer with four very good pitches. That can be difficult, because when you go to the mound, you're not sure which of your four pitches is going to be a good pitch that outing. If he ended up having an "out" pitch, it might have been his change-up. I always was amused by how many times Monty would close a game out by getting a strikeout with his change-up.

The other thing that needs to be mentioned regarding Montgomery is that he got so many saves with so many Royals teams that weren't all that great. If you look at his stats, he was saving about half of the team's wins, which is pretty impressive. Bad teams will do that for you, too.

A Defensive Gem

Monty made one of the best defensive plays of any pitcher in Royals history. One hitter grounded a high chopper back up the middle. Instinctively, Montgomery snapped his glove back behind him, the ball happened to go into the glove's pocket, and Monty threw to first for the out. It was strictly a luck play, but it's so much fun to see that on highlight reels now.

As with many of the other guys, off the field, Monty is a guy of many interests and very smart. He was good to interview and very thoughtful regarding his profession. If you asked him questions about things, you'd always get a complete thought.

Monty always liked to have the latest electronic gadget. He was intrigued by all that stuff. He's just a fascinating guy of many interests.

CLASS OF 2004

Denny Matthews

I was startled to learn shortly after the 2003 season that I would be inducted into the Royals Hall of Fame, class of 2004. Sure, I had thought about it in recent years, particularly when David Glass and others started discussing the possibility of my induction into the Baseball Hall of Fame in Cooperstown. Still, the Hall of Fame, whether for the club or baseball as a whole, is not something you dwell on.

In November 2003, the Royals announced my induction at a press conference. That's when it really hit me that it was reality. Jeff Montgomery told me something that day, though, that stuck with me. He said: "As neat as the press conference was, the full impact won't hit you until the evening of the induction." He was right on.

Looking back, there were so many things about the night that would be special alone, but to have them together is overwhelming. And it's really impossible for me to pick out one highlight of the night. Before the ceremony, I was brought in from the right-field bullpen in a car, and wheeled around the stadium. As we circled the warning track, there were about eight to 10 Anaheim Angel players in their dugout, clapping—which was cool.

For my big night, Fred White was the emcee, and Herk Robinson did the actual induction. It was special having each of them involved in that way. During the ceremony there was a highlight video with some of my calls and comments from some of the Royals greats, such as George Brett and Frank White. Afterwards, I threw out "first" pitches to each of my three brothers, which was extraordinary for all four of us. Then, the next day, manager Tony Peña signed the lineup card and gave it to me.

When the ceremony ended, David Glass allowed us to use the owner's suite for a celebration with friends and family. It gave me a chance to thank a lot of people who have been instrumental in my career and old friends that I hadn't seen in a while. The number of people that came from all over really stunned me. Pretty much everyone who was invited attended. That was really cool and made it extremely special because, in addition to my family and friends I've made around the Kansas City area, people I had grown up with also made the trip.

As part of the festivities, the Royals gave away a bobblehead of me that included a few of the top calls from my career. I didn't know what to think about that when they first told me about it, but it turned out to be really cool. Everybody who came up to the suite really got a kick out of the bobblehead.

The night went by too fast. I savored it, but it was a whirlwind. There were so many people and so much going on that it was hard to enjoy at that minute. But the memories from that night have stuck with me.

The whole thing still blows me away. To think: I was one of the very, very lucky few who broke in at the Major League level. I never called minor-league games as so many broadcasters do at the beginning of their career. It just happened that the Royals were an expansion team looking for a young broadcaster to work with the seasoned Buddy Blattner. I couldn't plan the timing of everything any better than that. The Royals situation was perfect, and it's worked out beautifully.

CLASS OF 2005

Bret Saberhagen

Bret Saberhagen pitched beyond his age (20) and experience in 1985. His control was so good at such a young age, even when he came up to the big club in 1984 at the age of 19. Sabes had a great fastball that he could spot. He also just knew how to pitch. He was instinctive. Some guys have a feel for the game. Bret certainly did. He also was exceptional defensively.

Saberhagen, at that age, with no more experience than he had, became the No. 1 guy in 1985. To put things in perspective, in '85, Sabes was about seven months *younger* than Zack Greinke, when Greinke made his debut in 2004.

"We were roommates on the road and in town during our first couple years. In town, we lived down at the Plaza. We had a great time together. One night we went down to the little jazz club at Plaza III to get a drink after a game, and he got carded. Obviously he wasn't quite old enough. It was funny as heck to me because here's this guy who was going to be taking us to the playoffs, but he couldn't get a beer. I was just 21, so I got a good laugh out of that."

—*Mark Gubicza*

Saberhagen carried on the club's great tradition of No. 1 starters, going back to the early 1970s with Steve Busby. Sabes, in my opinion, really took the pressure off the other four guys on that staff. They really fed off each other, but as the No. 1 guy, you wouldn't have guessed that he was 20 years old, because he had the poise, confidence, and selfishness needed on the mound. He also had great control and really good stuff, along with a solid idea of pitching. He wasn't a thrower; he was a pitcher.

Saberhagen showed as much confidence in himself during the 1985 World Series as anybody I saw—even at 20 years old. But he had the equipment to go along with it. I don't know if the equipment gave him the confidence or the confidence enhanced the equipment, or a combination of both. Regardless, it's safe to say that he had a carefree attitude. Saberhagen thrived in the environment produced with that pitching staff, and he was a terrific pitcher for us.

After going 2-0 with a 0.50 ERA in the World Series, Sabes was picked as the Series's Most Valuable Player.

During his eight years with the Royals, Sabes became the club's only two-time Cy Young Award winner, taking the honor in 1985 and '89.

Act Your Age

In addition to being a great pitcher that added a lot of life on the field, Saberhagen was a well-known prankster. In a few baseball movies, there's oftentimes a player who lights another player's spikes on fire...when the victim is wearing the shoes! That was one of Bret's favorites. He also used to enjoy tricking guys into squeezing a wad of tobacco in their hands, thinking it was a rock. He just enjoyed having a good time, trying to keep guys loose.

But things didn't always work out as planned. Don't take my word for it, though.

"Yeah, a couple of his jokes backfired against him. There was a time when Bo Jackson was wearing a suit and Sabes threw a grape or a strawberry that got on Bo's suit. Bo was really upset. He wasn't a good guy to have mad at you. He was willing, ready, and able to make Sabes part of the wall.

"Another one happened on a terribly hot Sunday afternoon when I was pitching. I finished the game and Sabes came up to throw a big bucket of ice water on me. It missed me and hit Jose Martinez, our first base coach. I think the ice shocked Jose so much that he just lost it. He wanted to get ahold of Sabes. Sabie had a blast, and he wasn't selective in his craziness, that's for sure."

—*Mark Gubicza*

Sabes and Gooby came along about the time that I stopped hanging out with the players. Just seeing that group in public, though, it's obvious that they were close and had a great time away from the field, which might've helped translate into wins on the field.

Ewing Kauffman

Muriel Kauffman

Joe Burke

Dick Howser

Whitey Herzog

George Brett

Hal McRae

Frank White

Amos Otis

Cookie Rojas

ORIGINAL PAINTINGS BY JOHN MARTIN. PRINTS COURTESY OF THE KANSAS CITY ROYALS.

John Mayberry

Willie Wilson

Fred Patek

Dan Quisenberry

Dennis Leonard

ORIGINAL PAINTINGS BY JOHN MARTIN. PRINTS COURTESY OF THE KANSAS CITY ROYALS.

Jeff Montgomery

Steve Busby

Larry Gura

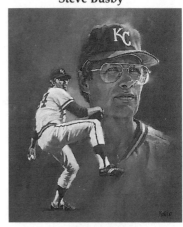

Paul Splittorff

Denny Matthews

Bret Saberhagen

ORIGINAL PAINTINGS BY JOHN MARTIN. PRINTS COURTESY OF THE KANSAS CITY ROYALS.

Chapter
6
THE MEN
IN ROYAL BLUE

Ted Abernathy

Ted Abernathy was a veteran reliever, a submarine-style pitcher like Dan Quisenberry. He also was a very southern gentleman type from North Carolina. He would tell me about life 12-15 years earlier, when he had broken in. Since I was just starting, that was a lot of fun.

He had a lot of big-league experience before he came to the Royals in 1970. He basically was at the end of his career by the time he got to us, but he was a good reliever for the club and our first true closer.

It's interesting that many people figure Quiz was the Royals' first submarine-style pitcher, but it was Abby.

Jerry Adair

Even though he was one of the least likely candidates, Jerry Adair hit the first inside-the-park home run in Royals history. Jerry was not at all fast, but he was a superb fielder with great hands. He didn't have much range, but knew how to play positions. Jerry had a really light complexion, so he was given the nickname of "the ghost."

Jerry's inside-the-park homer came on April 23, 1969, at Municipal Stadium against Seattle. (Ironically, Marty Pattin was the Seattle pitcher.) Inside-the-park home runs are always exciting to see, but particularly so with guys you wouldn't expect one from.

Willie Aikens

Willie Aikens came to us from the then-California Angels in December of 1979 as a first baseman. He was a very slow runner, but he had a quick bat. He and Tony Solaita probably were two of the strongest guys ever to play for the Royals. Willie was a great offensive force for us even though he was so slow on the bases.

As a first baseman, Willie was adequate. I remember a play in Detroit. Dan Quisenberry was trying to finish up the game and had a one-run lead. Kirk Gibson hit a slow ground ball up the first base line, in fair territory. Aikens came in and then was mesmerized by the ball. He just watched it and then let it go. It very slowly went foul. Willie could have picked it up and tagged Gibby or stepped on the bag. Instead, he let it go foul. Who knows why. (You know what's coming next.) Gibson hit a line drive that tore out about three rows of seats in the upper deck, and we lost the game. The thing sounded like a gunshot going off.

Willie had a very good postseason in 1980. He batted .400 and hit four homers during the World Series against Philadelphia.

Willie's a nice guy, even though he is in prison. There wasn't anything criminal or nasty in his disposition or personality, but he got on the wrong track and got hung up with some bad people.

Luis Alcaraz

Luis Alcaraz came to the Royals from the Los Angeles Dodgers in 1969. Buddy Blattner and I were working one of our first spring training games that year. Luis came to bat, and neither one of us was that familiar with him. Pretty much all we knew was that he had been with the Dodgers organization.

When Luis came up to bat, Buddy inadvertently said, "Here is one of the Royals' new additions, Luis Alcatraz." He caught it right away, and then corrected it and spelled it out. Then I said, "You should have known better than to call Luis Alcaraz, Luis Alcatraz, for you should know that no man is an island." That was one of my first early bad puns. Bud responded, "Oh, man. It's much too early to start that."

Kevin Appier

Kevin Appier always had great stuff and a good arm. He had games where he was dominant. His slider was so good that right-handed batters didn't want any part of it. He had a tendency to throw a lot of pitches, which hurt him in the later innings of a lot of games. He just wore himself down. His mechanics were unusual. I'm not sure you would ever take a video of Ape's delivery and use it as an example of great mechanics. For him, though, it worked. Sometimes you had to wonder how he avoided hurting his arm.

On the mound he was flopping here and there, kicking and diving, sometimes falling, and the mound was torn up. He was fun to watch defensively because you never knew when he was going to dive headlong or slide along. He was a trip. He was a smart guy, very personable and funny with a quirky sense of humor. Moonman and Planet Appier were his nicknames. Unusual personality. He has a farm south of Kansas City. He gets on his bulldozer and does his own landscaping.

Luis Aquino

Luis Aquino, a spot starter and reliever, didn't make a big impression on the Royals. Except for in one area ... music. I remember Luis as the player who popularized playing certain songs when he entered the game. He was the first to have his own song. The first time he did it, he didn't get anybody out. Maybe it didn't work out so well.

Steve Balboni

Steve "Bye-Bye" Balboni is one of the top five strongest guys ever to play for the Royals. He was a true power hitter and first baseman when the club needed one. In fact, he still has the team record for home runs in a year with 36 in 1985.

He also had one of the most unusual home runs ever hit at Royals Stadium. Late in the 1985 season, we were trying to jockey our way into first place. On a Sunday afternoon late in the game, Balboni hit a game-winning home run that he pulled foul down the left field line. It had a nice draw, like a golf ball, but when it got to the corner, it worked its way back into fair territory for a homer. It was a key home run in the season.

It was the most memorable home run, to me, that he hit. Nobody in the ballpark thought it would be fair. It was one of those magical things that happened in that magical year.

Besides being a great power hitter for the Royals, Steve was a great card player. He would come to the ballpark at noon to play cards. Very soft-spoken, very nice, but not easy to get to know. Once you did get to know him, you could have great conversations with him. Very bright, good personality, good sense of humor, and very popular with his teammates.

Tim Belcher

Tim Belcher brought a toughness to the pitching staff. He was a very competitive, hard-nosed, go at 'em type of pitcher. He would throw as hard as he could and challenge hitters.

Tim was a great student of the game. He was kind of a rabble rouser, but in a good way. He brought a good attitude and toughness to the team that we hadn't had in a while.

Belch and I had an intriguing conversation in the late 1990s when people were talking about how the major leagues were starting to use "juiced" baseballs. He said, "There was a time when I could get a ball back from the umpire and I could take my thumb and press into the skin of the ball between the seams, and I could make an indentation. Now every time I get a ball back from the umpire, I will press into the thing and it's like pressing into a golf ball. You can't get any kind of indentation. You tell me they haven't juiced up the balls. Don't tell me it is an isolated thing. I have done that all over the country. These balls are rock hard. The seams used to be raised a little bit, but now they are so tight, there is no differential between the seams and the rest of the ball. They are down into the ball, and it is harder to get a grip. Now it is harder to make the ball do what you want it to do."

He was the first guy to point out to me that they were doing something with the ball. I thought that was a fabulous observation. I began to suspect something like that a long time ago! Belch just further confirmed it.

Carlos Beltran

Carlos Beltran signed with and was developed by the Royals. It has been interesting to see him mature both on and off the field. He was extremely reserved and withdrawn early, which I think had a lot to do with him being uncomfortable with his English. Each subsequent year, he seems more relaxed with everybody. Now he is more outgoing, expressing himself very well.

Carlos has great ability and a great feel for the game. That's a superb but rare combination. He is a tremendous base stealer. He reminds many people of Amos Otis by the way he approaches the game. He is smooth and controlled, just like A.O. The perception is that he is not trying or going all out, but he is, believe me. Again, just like A.O. But similar to the former Royals Hall of Fame center fielder, Carlos plays hard and smart, which sometimes is misinterpreted. I have seldom seen him not hustle.

"I think it's unfair to compare different generations. Technology is different than it was when I played. Players are stronger, they have computers to help study hitters or pitchers, and the balls are supposed to be juiced now. It's unfair to guys like Carlos. It was unfair to compare me to older players. If Hank Aaron had exercised like they do today, there's no telling how many homers he would have hit. Babe Ruth played during the 'dead ball' era, and he still hit more than 60 home runs. How would he do today?

"In regard to how some people said that it looked like I was loafing because I made plays look so easy, inside, I was working twice as hard to get to the ball, but people couldn't see it. I ran easy, so I guess it looked easy. I suppose that's the same way it is with Beltran."

—*Amos Otis*

But how does he compare to Amos Otis? Even though, much like Amos, I don't like comparing players, especially in different eras, I can see some similarities.

Defensively, no difference. Both had above-average throwing arms. Their speed is similar. Both have great base-stealing ability. (Although Amos still has the record for most stolen bases in one game, five, against the Brewers in 1971.) They can steal any time they want. Offensively, very similar. Both could hit for average, although Beltran might have the slight edge, possibly due to the fact that he's a switch hitter. Both could bunt. Both could hit in the clutch. Power, the same. Build, kind of the same. Beltran might be thicker. And they are similar as people—you have to get to know them both before they are comfortable. Pretty comparable.

But, again, it's somewhat unfair and impossible to compare because you're comparing a young, gifted player with potential to one of the greatest Royals of all time.

Juan Berenguer

Juan Berenguer was an emotional pitcher with as good a fastball as any Royals pitcher ever. "Señor Smoke" gave up the hardest home run ever authored by a Royals pitcher. When Dave Winfield was with the Yankees, he hit a shot off Berenguer in front of a capacity crowd at Kauffman Stadium. Berenguer threw a pitch as hard as he could, and Winfield hit it as hard as he could. Winfield pulled it down the left field line. The ball was hit so hard that a 10-year-old kid stuck his hand out trying to get the souvenir and the ball broke his hand. It was a blur. I think the ball took .9 seconds to get from the bat to the boy's hand. It was a rocket. It was not the longest, but probably the hardest, homer ever at Royals Stadium.

Kurt Bevacqua

"Dirty Kurt" Bevacqua was loud, fun, outgoing and animated. Kurt was competitive, played hard and played many different positions. He would find a way to get his uniform dirty, no matter what he did. Even sitting in the dugout. If he didn't play, we would go back to the clubhouse after a game and his uniform would be dirty.

I remember one afternoon, he and I were walking back to our hotel in Minneapolis after going out to lunch. (We both were single.) A convertible came down the street, with two good-looking girls inside. Kurt yelled at them, asking if they wanted to go to the game. About that time, the traffic started moving. So, Kurt started running after the car, and dove into the back seat. I don't know if I was more awestruck or dumbfounded, but I just stood there on the sidewalk.

"Dirty" Kurt and I decided at a Royals reunion in August 1988 that we're too old to have any more adventures together. *Photo courtesy of Denny Matthews*

I didn't see Kurt again until we got to the ballpark. I asked him what happened. He said, "They are coming to the game, and then we're all going out afterwards." I couldn't believe it! That was the easiest date I ever got in my life.

He was funny and a great person to hang out with. There are a ton of Bevacqua stories out there. He would stir things up. He was very colorful. He rubbed some people the wrong way, but I liked him.

Doug Bird

Doug Bird had an interesting personality, which may have helped cause some flak between him and Whitey. They used to go round and round. In Boston one time, Whitey told him, "If you get 0 and two on any hitter, I don't want the ball to come near home plate." He got ahead of a hitter 0-2, and the next pitch nearly hit Fred and me in the booth. It almost came into the booth. That was Birdie's way of saying no one was going to touch this pitch, and "Here you go, Whitey, how's this for not close to the plate!"

Bird was used as a starter and reliever. He had good stuff. At times he was really good. Whitey would tell you that Birdie's concentration was not A-1 at all times, which might have been the one thing that prevented him from being better than he was. Still, he was a good, useful pitcher for a lot of years.

Ken Brett

I remember a spring training game in Ft. Myers, when Ken Brett was pitching for the White Sox, facing his younger brother George. He served one up that George blasted over the center field fence. Everyone had a lot of fun with that.

Ken was with us only during 1980-81, but it was a fun time. I think he and George really enjoyed it. Kemmer (which was his real name) was as competitive as George, and many say he was a better athlete.

Ken broke in with the Red Sox at the age of 19 and pitched in the World Series that season. He remains one of the youngest players to appear in the World Series.

Kemmer lost his battle with cancer in the fall of 2003.

Nelson Briles

Nelson Briles was an entertainer. He would throw a pitch and land on his stomach. That would happen two or three times in an inning. It was hilarious. He put so much into the pitch that he ended up flat on his belly. (Hmmm, Nellie on his belly…)

Nellie had a great sense of humor. One of his tricks was sounding eerily like a Volkswagen horn. We'd be on the bus, and he'd break out his VW honking noise. The bus driver would look around at all of his mirrors, to no avail. He never could figure out who was honking.

Nellie, who had some good years with the Cardinals and Pirates, now works in the front office for the Pirates in community affairs and group sales.

Paul Byrd

Paul Byrd had a great 2002 season for the Royals, which turned out to be his only season in Kansas City. He was an interesting guy to talk to. He gave a lot of thought to pitching—mechanics, setting up hitters, etc. I have the feeling that he will be a good pitching coach one day if he so chooses.

Paul is a thoughtful, insightful, smart person. Everybody from his teammates to the media to the fans liked him. He worked hard, and you knew that when he went to the mound, he was going to give you quality innings.

Byrd connected with the fans as well as any player we have ever had. He recognized them, he enjoyed that relationship, and he cultivated it to a degree. In fact, he had a loyal upper deck following at Kauffman Stadium that became known as the Byrd's Nest. There was one particularly hot afternoon game that he pitched, and he sent bottles of water up to that group of fans. Now tell me, how many players—in any era, not just in today's game—would do something like that during the game? Not many.

After the 2002 season he chose to go back to the Atlanta Braves, a team he had played with before coming to Kansas City. He and his family liked it here, and the fans obviously wish that he would have stayed, but he didn't. That's part of the game. It's a shame that he left, because I think he would have gone down as one of the most popular players in the history of this franchise.

David Cone

David Cone is the local boy who got away. Although he pitched well for the Royals, he had his best years elsewhere. Coney was a great competitor with all kinds of pitches. He would throw any pitch from any angle, which made him interesting. He threw that sidearm thing, which he called Loredo.

David was a free spirit. One of his tricks was when we were on the charter plane, he would sit in the very back, and when the plane would land, and the wheels would hit, he would go shooting down the aisles on two magazines like a surfer. You always want to see one of your top pitchers flying down the aisle. He did other things we can't put in the book.

Al Cowens

Al Cowens worked himself out of a tough part of Los Angeles and became a very good player. He is one of the most underrated players in

Royals history. That's partially because of the way he played, partially because of the other names on the team, and partially because of his personality. Al was very quiet and low-key. He didn't stand out in a crowd.

He was a smart and complete player, but his tools were subtle. He ran faster than it appeared. He had more power than it appeared. And he possessed a better arm than it appeared. A telling comment came from George Brett after a game when Cowens threw out a runner at third from right field. A reporter asked George how Al made such an accurate throw. Brett's comment was simply, "Well, Al Cowens threw it."

Al Cowens passed away in March 2002.

Steve Crawford

Former pitcher Steve Crawford, who came to the Royals from Boston, was nicknamed Shag after umpire Shag Crawford. He had a great personality and was really popular with the other players. Everyone liked to say "Shag" in a deep voice.

Shag and George Brett went to a hockey game at Kemper Arena one night, and they sat about three rows behind the benches. During the tied game, somebody deflected the puck into the stands, and it hit Shag in the head. It didn't even faze him.

Fred White hosted a golf tournament in Wichita every year after the season. Each year they had an auction and a dinner the night before. Some of the guys would hit the Wichita hot spots that night after the dinner. One year, my hotel room was next to Shag's. A commotion in the hallway woke me up around 2:15. I heard a loud voice say, "I can't find my keys!" It was Shag. He made a couple of strange noises, and then busted down his door. The rest of the night, I kept hearing sounds like Shag was clearing his throat. I don't think that's what he was really doing…but he kept at it the rest of the night. And I wasn't the only one who heard it. We all knew why he was groggy the next morning, but everybody had a good laugh about that night.

Bruce Dal Canton

Bruce Dal Canton came to the Royals as part of the Freddie Patek-Jerry May trade when we sent Bob Johnson to the Pirates. He wasn't an overwhelming pitcher for the Royals, but he was a contributor. There was a stretch where Bruce, Steve Mingori, and a couple other relievers hadn't pitched in several games. As our bus was leaving Detroit one morning, we went through an industrial area, where a sign read "Detroit Cold Storage." Mingo turned to Dal Canton and said, "Bruce, we should stop the bus and see if we can get our arms out of storage."

Moe Drabowsky

Moe, who was born in Poland, was the winning pitcher in the Royals' first game ever. A few years before coming here, while with the Chicago Cubs, Moe gave up Stan Musial's 3,000th hit at Wrigley Field.

Moe Drabowsky, well-known prankster and winning pitcher in the Royals' first game in April 1969. *Photo courtesy of the Kansas City Royals*

Moe Drabowsky was one of the true characters in the Royals organization. Throughout his career he was famous for his pranks. His best known joke was when he put goldfish in the opposing bullpen's water cooler. One of my favorites was when he'd get the phone number for the opposing bullpen, and he would call the other bullpen and get one of their pitchers warming up. That team's manager would see he had a pitcher warming up, so he'd call and tell the guy to sit down. A few minutes later, Moe would call down there again and get the same pitcher warming up. The manager would get ticked off and call back down there to tell the pitcher to sit down. This would go on for two or three innings before someone would figure out that it was Moe.

Jim Eisenreich

John Schuerholz took a chance with Jim Eisenreich, who had Tourrette's Syndrome. Many fans jeered at him at opposing parks. No one really knew much about Tourrette's at the time, so baseball people didn't think he could overcome it. It was a distraction to Jim and his teammates with Minnesota. But Jim came here and began taking a medication that helped him control the symptoms. Fans in Kansas City really embraced Jim for overcoming the disease.

On the field, Jim became a very good outfielder. He might be the best judge of fly balls the Royals ever have had. The Royals had a spring training game at the Houston Astros' complex in Florida. The wind was blowing between 40 and 50 miles per hour. Every fly ball was an adventure. Jim was playing center field. He made several catches that day, never missing a step.

Today, Jim still lives in the Kansas City area, where he remains active in the fight against Tourrette's Syndrome.

Al Fitzmorris

Pitcher Al Fitzmorris was a converted outfielder from the Chicago White Sox. Fitzy was an excellent sinkerballer. Ironically, Fitzmorris, who was a switch hitter, was the first player in Royals history to get a hit from each side of the plate in one game.

What Did He Say?

On the mound, Fitzy worked slowly. He was famous for just messing around on the mound. One night, in fact, his slow pace got me in trouble. During my second year, I was still trying to figure out how to be a big-league announcer. We were in Milwaukee and it was a Friday night, two days before the 4th of July, a big holiday weekend. We have commercial drop-ins during each game that you slip in between pitches or batters, or whenever possible. Ed Shepard, our producer-engineer, handed me the card that said "Guy's Foods drop-in."

Everybody in Kansas City knew about Guy's Foods. The card was in front of me, I was thinking about how they were a good sponsor, so I wanted to really pump them up. I started thinking about the holiday weekend, everybody out picnicking, boating, whatever. So I said, "For those of you planning a holiday picnic, we sure hope you take along plenty of those good Guy's potato chips." Fitzy was wasting time on the mound. I obviously had more time to fill, so I thought I would give Guy's another plug. And the next line out of my mouth was "And when you're in the store, be sure to grab Guy's nuts." I thought my career was over right then and there. I looked over at Buddy Blattner, and he looked like somebody had shot him.

When we got back from the road trip, Guy Caldwell, an older man in his 70s who founded Guy's Foods, was at the ballpark. I told him the story, thinking he might be upset about it. Instead, he thought that was one of the funniest things he ever heard.

Kirk Gibson

When Kirk Gibson arrived here in 1991, he brought his own particular swagger to the team, along with intensity and a fiery personality. While he was with Detroit, he hit one of the hardest home runs ever at Royals Stadium … one that went off the back wall of the right field bullpen. Gibson was a big hockey fan and a great football wide receiver at Michigan State.

One of my best memories of Gibson was on August 26, 1991, when Bret Saberhagen threw his no-hitter against the Chicago White Sox. Late in the game, with Gibson in left, there was a ball hit to left center. Gibson, who was left-handed, sprinted to the ball, and he tried to backhand it, but didn't make the catch. He got his glove on it, so it was ruled an error. It probably should have been ruled a hit. A little controversial, but Sabes went on to get his no-hitter.

And Your Mama Wears Combat Boots!

During spring training in Gibson's only year here, we had a game at Baseball City in Florida. There were only about 3,000 people in the stands. Gibby was on at second base. Somebody hit a ground ball, and

Typical Kirk Gibson—going all out.
Photo courtesy of the Kansas City Royals

Gibby should have gone to third, but he didn't. The next hitter grounded the ball to second, and Gibby moved up to third. Some guy in the seats yelled at Gibson, "You should have been there an out ago!" Gibby's head snapped around, and he shouted, "Shut the f--- up!" We could hear it perfectly in the booth. So much for making friends with the fans early.

What's Your Name, Little Boy?

Another time, Gibby brought his little boy down to the field for batting practice in Kansas City. Little Gibby, who was about five years old, was wearing a uniform. Cute kid. Fred White and I were around the batting cage, Gibby was hitting, and Fred noticed Little Gibby holding a bat in his hand. When Gibson was done hitting, he came around, and Fred said to the little boy, "How are you doing?" The little kid just looked at him. So Fred said, "What's your name?" The little kid didn't say anything. Finally, Gibby snapped at his son, "Tell him your G--d--- name!"

Tom Gordon

Tom Gordon had one of the best curveballs that the Royals had ever developed. Unfortunately, he had control problems early in his career, and he was used as both a starter and a reliever. Since leaving the Royals in 1995, he has had some good years as a closer.

Are Those Firestone or Goodyear?

We were in Minnesota at the end of a long road trip, getting ready to leave the hotel on a Sunday morning. The luggage truck was sitting in front of the bus, and everybody was trickling out of the hotel and onto the bus. The guys' luggage was going onto the truck—mainly suitcases and hanging bags. All of a sudden, one of the bellmen rolls out a flatbed cart that has four tires on it! He puts the tires on the team bus. Somebody leans out of the bus and says, "Are you sure that goes on the truck?" The bellmen said it did. "One of your players had these in his room," he explained. They belonged to Gordon. He had purchased four tires in Chicago. Nobody ever asked why.

Mark Gubicza

Former pitcher Mark Gubicza is one of my favorite Royals. He was a favorite of his teammates and one of the important pieces of the puzzle for the Royals in the 1980s. He was one of the club's best ever and deserves to be in the team's Hall of Fame.

Gooby was a big hockey fan, so he and I always would bet on the Stanley Cup playoffs. He was from Philadelphia, so he was a big Flyers fan. He then moved to Los Angeles and became a Kings fan. We talked baseball 10 percent of the time and hockey 90 percent of the time. We had some great hockey debates!

Mark Gubicza was always one of my favorite Royals and a great hockey fan.
Photo courtesy of the Kansas City Royals

Read the Letters, Starting at the Top

Gubicza's name reads like an eye chart. During spring training we went over to Pompano Beach to play the Texas Rangers. Pompano Beach had an old, rickety ballpark. It was made completely of wood. (This was the stadium where, about a week before we went over there, Pete Incaviglia hit a line drive through the wooden fence. All the guys had to look at the hole in the fence.)

The stadium looked like it tipped one way. Regardless, the press box was on top of this old deck, and it would sway in the wind. Our booth was tiny, with the public address announcer in the booth next to us. The partition between us was a piece of plywood about one-sixteenth of an inch thick. Gooby was starting that day, and about 10 minutes before the game, the PA guy stuck his head in the door, and said, "I think I got all your guys' names down, but how do you pronounce this pitcher's name?" I pronounced it for him. He practiced a few times while he stood there, but he just could not pronounce Gubicza. He left, and we could hear him practicing in the next booth. A few times he got it right. A couple of minutes before the game, the PA guy goes through the lineup beautifully. He comes to Gooby and says, "And pitching for the Royals. Mark Garbonzo." So much for the pronunciation lesson.

Jack Hernandez

Jackie Hernandez, who came to the Royals from the Twins in the expansion draft, was our first shortstop. He was a good defensive shortstop, but he didn't have much pop in his bat. Jackie also spoke clear English. While Jackie was here (1969-70), we had a little utility infielder named Juan Rios, who didn't play much and really couldn't speak English very well.

During an August game in 1969, Rios played to give someone a rest. In the game, Rios got a couple of hits and drove in a couple runs, and we won the game. I was doing the pregame show with Buddy Blattner at the time. By that time in the season, the Royals were far out of the race and we had interviewed nearly everyone on the team…except Rios.

On my way to the ballpark, I had the idea that I would interview Juan. I figured Juan might never get on the pregame show if it wasn't after a game when he got a couple hits and drove in a couple runs. So even though Juan didn't understand much English, Jackie had helped him along all season, and I thought I would use Jackie as an interpreter. Juan and Jackie agreed to it, so along with our producer-engineer Ed Shepherd, we all met down the right field line to tape the interview. I was afraid we would get only three or four words out of Juan, and I was really sweating it.

Shep started the tape, and I said, "Our guest tonight on the Royals' pregame show is Juan Rios, who drove in a couple of runs last night in the Royals' 5-2 victory. Juan doesn't speak or understand English, but Jackie Hernandez has graciously consented to be our interpreter." Then I said to Jackie, "Ask Juan his impressions and his feelings about the game last night, about his big night." I put the microphone in front of Jackie, who asked Juan the question. Juan's eyes lit up, so I put the microphone in front of Rios and he started chattering away in Spanish. I thought how this was very cool and it's working. Jackie was nodding his head and smiling. And Juan's smiling and yapping. Then they'd both laugh and keep talking. Juan was on a roll. I knew we had it made. Juan stopped and looked at Jackie and smiled. So I put the mike in front of Jackie to get the interpretation. Jackie looked at me and said, "Juan said he feel pretty good."

Are you kidding me? Juan just gave us his life story, he talked so long. I don't know exactly how we made that four and a half minutes work, but somehow they worked. I guess I'll never know what great, or at least long, answer Juan gave.

David Howard

David Howard, who was with the Royals during 1991-97, was a very good athlete and actually one of the best golfers the Royals have ever had. He was a switch hitter who could play anywhere defensively.

Many Royals fans will remember David as the victim of one of the greatest catches in baseball history and certainly the greatest catch that I ever have seen. Jim Edmonds was playing center field for the Angels in a game at Kauffman Stadium. David hit a ball to dead center. Edmonds, with his back to the infield, ran as hard as he could toward the center field wall. He didn't have any type of angle toward the ball and couldn't possibly see the ball, but he laid out, reached out as far as he could with his glove, and caught the ball while hitting the warning track. I don't know how many catches could be any better than that. Sure, there is a lot of luck involved, but the degree of difficulty on that thing was amazing. If you're going straight back without any angle, it's physically impossible to get your head back over your shoulders enough to see the ball coming.

In Jim's mind's eye, he had to figure the ball was somewhere in that vicinity coming down, and when he laid out he got his hands and his glove out there where he thought it might come down, and it did. Then he held onto it, which is another degree of difficulty. Yeah, when you say David Howard, you probably should say Jim Edmonds in the same breath.

Al Hrabosky

Hungo, the "Mad Hungarian," pitched for the Royals during 1978-79. He was a fun guy with a great sense of humor. On the mound he was a fierce competitor who would go at the hitter with his fastball. And then he had his routine, which was amusing.

This was his first go-round in the American League. Hungo's routine was this thing behind the mound where he'd meditate and then slam the ball into his glove. Then, with a scowl on his face, he'd come storming up the hill from the back side of the mound. He'd glare in to the catcher, glare at the hitter, and then go to work.

The Mad Hungarian, Al Hrabosky, on one of his good days. *Photo courtesy of the Kansas City Royals*

One night shortly after Hrabosky joined us, we were playing a game in Minnesota. He went through his routine two or three times. Bill Kunkel, who was a former major league pitcher, was umpiring second base that night. He went over toward Hrabosky and started talking to him. We had no idea what they were talking about. Later we found out that Kunkel told Hrabosky that he couldn't do his routine. Hungo said, "What do you mean I can't do that? I've been doing this in the other league."

"I know you have, but now you're in the American League," Kunkel replied.

Hrabosky fired back, "That doesn't make any difference. There is no rule against what I am doing. It's perfectly legal."

Kunkel wasn't too happy about that. He said, "I just made up a rule and you can't do it any more. And if you do it, I'll throw you out of the game. How about that!"

Since we didn't know that was going on, I don't remember whether Hungo did his routine any more that night. But, that was his introduction to the American League, or at least his introduction to Bill Kunkel.

It Didn't Need a Stewardess, But It Was Hit Fairly Far

Ron Fairly was finishing up his career with the Angels when Hungo and the Royals made a stop in Anaheim. Fairly, who was a great fastball hitter, came in as a pinch hitter. Well, of course, Hungo was brought in from the bullpen. It was his first time pitching there. There was a big crowd, and they were wild, especially when Hrabosky came in.

Fairly was standing casually off to the side with the bat on his shoulder, watching Hungo come in from the pen. Hungo went through his warmups, and the crowd was going goofy with Hungo on the mound.

When Hungo was done with his warmup tosses, Fairly stepped into the batter's box and dug in. Meanwhile, Hrabosky went through his routine behind the mound. He thought for a moment, slammed the ball in his glove, turned around, stormed up the back of the mound and peered in at Fairly. By this time, the crowd was absolutely howling.

Hungo's first pitch, of course, was a fastball. Fairly hit it about 28 miles.

After all that build-up, it was as if Fairly said, "Oh, that's very nice, but I love fastballs, thank you very much." He absolutely bashed one, and that was the end of that.

The Fu-Man-Chu

Jerry Coleman, who broadcasts for San Diego, is known for his malapropisms. When Hungo was with the Cardinals, they were playing the Padres in San Diego. Hrabosky, who always had some type of facial hair, finished his warmups in the bullpen, and Jerry Coleman said, "And now out of the Cardinals bullpen, here comes Al Hrabosky looking menacing and fierce in his fu-man-chu haircut."

Bo Jackson

Aside from the obvious on the field, Bo Jackson was one of the best players around kids that I have ever seen. He related to kids beautifully. They loved him. Even as big as he was, if he thought a kid was intimidated at all, he had a knack of making them feel very much at ease. When one of my nephews was about six years old, my brother brought him to Milwaukee to see a series. Little Brett Matthews wanted to meet Bo Jackson. So I took him down to the dugout and I told Bo that Brett was down there and wondered if he would say hello and sign a ball for him. Bo said sure. So I brought Brett over and he was pretty intimidated. So Bo sat down and put little Brett on his lap. Brett immediately felt at ease, and we took a couple great photographs.

Bo had an incredible ability to make little kids feel at ease. It's obvious that he genuinely likes them, and I think kids pick up on that.

Bo was a guy not only of many talents but of many interests. He was fun to talk to about other stuff. It's evident today that he's had varied interests. He lives up near Chicago around Coghill Golf Course, running his own business and doing speaking engagements. He's also involved in several charities. Aside from the obvious things that everybody always talks about, that's another side of him that isn't mentioned enough.

Was that Josh Gibson?

The speed that Bo could generate and the power that he could generate as a hitter were the two things that really stood out. After signing Bo, the Royals brought him to Kansas City for batting practice, before he was to report in the minor leagues at Memphis. It was obvious that Bo had "easy power"—he would swing smoothly and the ball just kept going. When a lot of guys hit the ball hard, it goes for a ways and then begins to descend. When Bo made contact, the ball kept carrying.

Negro Leagues legend Buck O'Neil made a similar comment. Buck has said numerous times that he was in the stadium and heard a tremendous crack of the bat. He says that he didn't know who it was, but he had to go find out because he hadn't heard that sound since the powerful Josh Gibson of the old Negro Leagues. (Buck tells the story in a much more romantic and dramatic way.)

"Bo is the greatest athlete I have ever seen in a baseball uniform. He could hit a ball farther, throw a ball farther, and run faster than any human being I have ever seen in a baseball uniform. It was a coup for us to sign Bo Jackson."

—John Schuerholz

Despite being a right-handed hitter, Bo's speed to first rivaled that of any left-handed hitter. He frequently made a routine ground ball to short a very close play at first. It's a shame that things didn't turn out better with his hip.

Wally Joyner

The Royals have had some very good defensive first basemen, including a couple of others in this book, Mike Fiore and John Mayberry. But with all due respect to those guys and other former Royals first basemen, Wally Joyner was the smoothest-fielding first baseman I've ever seen. He also was one of the best-throwing first basemen ever to play in the big leagues. Because of that, he never hurried or rushed a play. He was a lot of fun to watch.

In a quiet way, he was a team leader. A player doesn't assume that role immediately by joining a new team; it sort of evolves over time. But it was obvious on the field and in the clubhouse that the guys respected Wally.

We've All Been There and Done That

We were in Milwaukee for a series, getting ready to play on Sunday. The Shriners had a parade going down Wisconsin Avenue, which ran past the Pfister Hotel, which is where we were staying. We could see that the parade was going, seemingly, forever, and there was no way to get across Wisconsin Avenue. As with most parades, there were breaks here and there, but our bus driver didn't want to get involved.

The bus was already 20 minutes behind schedule. None of the coaches or managers was on the bus, so Wally decided to plop down in one of the first rows, normally occupied by the coaching staff. The guys were getting more and more impatient. So Wally very loudly announced, "Well, I'm going to put an end to this."

About that time he jumped out of his seat like a rocket, hit his head on the luggage rack, and damned near knocked himself cold. It was awful, but at the same time, it was hilarious. Needless to say, he didn't put an end to the parade, but he did make everyone change their focus for a few minutes.

That was one of the least smooth moves that Wally ever made.

Pat Kelly

Pat Kelly was an original expansion draft pick from Minnesota and gave the Royals the element of speed in 1969. He was a left-handed thrower and a left-handed hitter, and he was the most artistic, beautiful slider in Royals history. He had an incredible hook slide. (A hook slide is an old-fashioned and difficult slide where you hook your left foot or your right foot on the bag, depending where the throw is coming from the outfield.) It was fun to watch.

Patrick was a very congenial guy, and he had a beautiful voice. His speaking voice was a wonderful, soft, mellow sound. He also had an engaging smile.

When Pat emerged with the Royals, it was the big-leagues' first look at him. He was in obscurity with the Twins. Since he was relatively unknown, he used to get things in the mail from different Irish groups wanting to check on family background. Pat, who's an African American, got a big kick out of that because, of course, his ancestry probably didn't originate in Ireland.

Pat had a few good years with the Royals before playing for other teams, including Baltimore. He also became a very religious person. I've heard the story about when Patrick was with the Orioles and feisty Earl Weaver was the manager. One day, Earl and Pat were having a discussion. Among other things, religion came up. Pat asked Weaver, "Skip, do you walk with the Lord?"

Earl replied, "Well, sometimes, but you know, Pat, I wish once in a while you would walk with the bases loaded."

Jose Lima

Jose Lima, who played part of the 2003 season and again in 2005 for the Royals, brought some energy, experience and enthusiasm to the pitching staff that wasn't there before. That's not to say that manager Tony Peña wasn't upbeat enough, but Jose was a player who had that and was encouraging to all the other guys.

He was quite a character. I refer to him as a "camera-seeking missile" because he never saw a camera—still or TV—that he didn't like. But that's just his personality; he's very flamboyant on and off the field.

That flamboyance even carries over away from the field. Lima was exceeded by only Michael Tucker in the way that he dresses. Both of those guys have some of the most unbelievable threads in the history of baseball. Lima had his own particular style, but the guys would rib him once in a while, saying, "Is that one of Tucker's throwaways?" or, "Is that one of Tucker's rejects you're wearing?" In typical Lima fashion (no pun intended), he rolled with the punches.

Mark Littell

Mark Littell was a right-handed farm boy from southern Missouri who had that funky delivery, funky motion, and good stuff, but he had trouble controlling it consistently. He was our closer. Many remember Littell as the pitcher who gave up the home run to Chris Chambliss that ended the 1976 American League playoffs against New York.

The Royals really never could decide whether Littell was a starter or a reliever. I think out of necessity he became a closer because he had good strikeout stuff. Looking at the history of Royals closers, they've usually been finesse guys. Dan Quisenberry, obviously, wasn't a power pitcher.

Jeff Montgomery was not a strikeout guy. So Littell was the closest thing the Royals had to a power closer until Mike MacDougal came on strong in 2003.

Mark was somewhat naïve when he came up. I think that's how he got the nickname "Country." Mark ended up marrying one of the Royals Stadium usherettes.

Mike Macfarlane

Mike Macfarlane played baseball with a hockey mentality. Maybe more so than any other baseball player I've seen. (As a hockey fan and recreational player, I mean that as a real compliment.) By it I mean he was one of the fiercest competitors on the field and one of the really good guys off the field. He was tough-minded with a tough body. You knew he would lead the team in getting hit by pitches almost every year. After games, he had these big welts all over his arms and shoulders. As a catcher, you know you're going to get some of those anyway, but he got half of his as a hitter.

He had the perfect mentality for a catcher. In all aspects— mentality, physical build and ability, emotionally—he was perfect. On top of that, he was popular with his teammates. That respect helped him go out to the mound and challenge a pitcher, or chew one out. He also wasn't afraid to go out and pat a guy on the back and encourage him. Mike had a knack for knowing what to say and when to say it. He liked to get into the heads of his pitchers.

Offensively, Mike had occasional power and was a smart hitter. He knew when to try to hit a long ball or when to try to go up the middle with a hit. Overall, he had a great feel for the game, which comes out in his broadcast work now. If he so chooses, I'm quite sure he could be a successful coach or manager.

Buck Martinez

Buck Martinez was a 20-year-old catcher when he joined the Royals in 1969. He also was involved in one of the most memorable plays for me in the club's 35 years. It was Buck's first major league game, in June, 1969. We were playing the Twins, and Buck, at the age of 20, had not developed into the physical specimen that he later became. Instead, he was kind of a scrawny little guy at age 20. Bob Allison, the former Kansas football player, was running the bases for the Twins. There was going to be a play at the plate. Allison barreled into Buck and knocked him six or seven feet. Allison absolutely annihilated Martinez. But Buck held onto the ball. Later in the game, he homered. That was Buck's debut as a Royal. He had a solid career, but that might have been one of the highlights of his playing days.

Bob Allison of the Twins slams into young Royals catcher Buck Martinez at home plate at Municipal Stadium. Buck held on to the ball. *Photo courtesy of the Kansas City Royals*

According to the 1970 Royals media guide:

"He was activated on June 17, used as a pinch hitter in both games of a doubleheader the next day against Oakland. He flied out the first time, singled on his next trip. He pinch hit two more times and then started for the first time June 28th against Minnesota. The second time at bat he hit a 415-foot home run off Dave Boswell. It made him one of the youngest players who ever homered in his first starting assignment. Also displayed a strong arm and twice blocked Twin runners for outs at the plate. The next afternoon he had three singles in four at-bats against the Twins."

Even at a young age, Buck was a cerebral thinker of the game. I don't think anybody realized at that time, obviously, that he was going to be a major league manager down the line and a good radio/TV commentator. But he was bright at a very young age, and he had a long, if not a spectacular, career as a big-league catcher.

Jerry May

Jerry May was in the trade with the Pirates in which Bruce Dal Canton and Freddie Patek came to Kansas City for Bob Johnson. That gave the Royals an experienced catcher. The one funny Jerry May story that comes to mind was from a trip to New York. There was a time when all of the teams traveling through New York stayed at the Americana Hotel. Evidently, some people knew that the teams stayed there, and there was a stretch of several robberies of players' rooms.

Jerry wasn't the best dresser on the team; he had some goofy-looking outfits. (Remember, this was the 1970s.) When Jerry got back to his room after a game, somebody had broken in and taken almost everything that he had. Almost everything. He had one of the ugliest pairs of these white, ankle-high boots—those ugly disco-type boots. The robbers took everything out of Jerry's room but left those ugly white boots in the room. That's the ultimate slap in the face ... or in the foot, I guess. Man, did the guys get on him for that.

Steve Mingori

Oh, Mingo! Steve Mingori was one of the guys I hung out with quite a bit in the "good old days." There are a lot of stories I can't tell. Mingo is a beauty.

B-U-L-L-P-E-N

The bullpen guys in those days were very close. The guys really got along well—Mingo, Doug Bird and Marty Pattin. They always had something going.

There was a time, however, when the bullpen guys felt that they weren't getting the attention or the credit that they thought they deserved. We were in Cleveland, and it was cold. Mingo took white tape and formed the letter "B" on the back of one of the pitchers' blue warmup jackets. Then, he took the tape and made a "U" on somebody else's jacket. Eventually, they spelled out "BULLPEN." Then he had all the guys come out of the dugout at the same time and walk toward the right-field bullpen. Mingo thought that was great.

Words of wisdom from Mingo ... always elicit a positive reaction.
Photo courtesy of Denny Matthews

You Can't Take It with You

Mingo, Bird and Pattin used to argue all the time about anything. It was ridiculous. One night, Mingo and Bird got into an argument about life insurance. People will try to sell a ballplayer anything. Some insurance guy got to Bird and sold him about $87 bajillion dollars worth of life insurance. He didn't need life insurance any more than he needed somebody to drill three holes in his right arm.

He was telling Mingo about this staggering amount he bought. Mingo replied, "Birdie, what in the hell. You don't need $87 bajillion dollars worth of life insurance." Of course, taking Mingo's verbal tirade, Birdie was very much on the defensive. He said, "Well, look what I get," and he told Mingo about the benefits. As they continued to go back and forth, Mingo eventually said, "Man, you are the dumbest guy I've ever met."

By that time, Birdie was totally frustrated. He started to go to the field, but before he left he stopped, turned around and yelled at Mingo, "Well, Mingo that's all you know about life insurance. The good news is that I get it all back when I die!"

Grease Is the Word

Marty Pattin always called Mingo, "Greasy Mingo." He'd say, "That greasy Italian Mingo." One year at spring training, either Bird or Pattin caught a huge fish out of the Gulf of Mexico. They took the fish out to the ballpark early before their workout, put it in Mingo's locker, and dressed it up. They put Mingo's hat on it and then hung a cigarette out of its mouth (Mingo was smoking at that time). They wanted it to look as much like Mingo as possible. It was classic.

Dave Morehead

Dave Morehead was one of our starting pitchers that first year. The Royals picked him in the second round of the expansion draft from Boston. He had a lot of arm problems; wildness and arm problems. Ray Boone, Bob Boone's father, signed Dave for Boston when he was 18 years old. (Dave actually went to the same high school in San Diego as Ray Boone and Ted Williams.)

During spring training of 1971, Dave started having a major problem finding the strike zone, similar to what happened with Steve Blass of the Pirates in 1973—although Blass's was more well-known, or at least was documented more in the media.

Dave couldn't even come close to home plate with a pitch of any kind. During one exhibition game at Terry Park, he started throwing to the catcher in warmups and he wasn't even coming close; I mean there were balls nine to 10 feet outside, balls seven or eight feet in front of the catcher, and a couple that went 10-12 feet over the catcher's head. You know how the home-plate umpire usually hangs around the plate when a pitcher's warming up? This particular day, the umpire cleared out, almost into the dugout. It was unbelievable.

Dave Nelson

Dave Nelson was basically a utility infielder for the Royals. (Although I believe when he was with Cleveland, he stole second, third, and home in the same game.) Davey was Whitey Herzog's designated DL guy. If Whitey had to get a pitcher on the team, or had to make a roster move, he would call Davey into the office and say, "Dave, we got to make a move here. We need a catcher bad because [so and so] is hurt. I want you to go out there and pull a hamstring tonight."

As prompted, Davey would pull a fake hammy and then they'd put him on the DL. Then Whitey could make his move with whatever he needed at that point in time. After the emergency had been resolved, Davey would come off the DL and he'd be active again until Whitey needed to make another move. Talk about being a utility player.

Nelson, who was with the Royals during 1976-77, has another distinction in the club's record books. While playing for the Texas Rangers, Davey was the first batter in Royals Stadium history, on April 10, 1973. He grounded out to pitcher Paul Splittorff. So, you guessed it … Davey also was the first out at Royals Stadium.

Roger Nelson

Roger "Spider" Nelson was the Royals' number-one draft choice in the expansion draft, from Baltimore. Roger had a good arm, but there wasn't room for him on Baltimore's loaded staff. He had some really good years in the minor leagues, which is where John Schuerholz saw him when John was with the Orioles. In turn, the Royals really liked his potential, and we drafted him number one.

Unfortunately, arm problems really slowed him down here. He was the Royals' workhorse for the first four months of the 1969 season, but then he had to take off two weeks for military duty with the Army National Guard. When he returned from military duty, he was experiencing some tightness in his shoulder. I'm not sure what he could do during two weeks of summer camp—maybe he wasn't throwing on a regular basis—it was kind of a squirrelly situation. It's a shame, because I think he could have been a very good pitcher.

In December 1972, the Royals traded Nelson and Richie Scheinblum to Cincinnati for Hal McRae and Wayne Simpson. Nelson, who was a hard worker and battler, returned to the Royals for one season in 1976.

"I hated that trade because I could see that this team was going to be good soon. But they needed a player like McRae. He was the key to making Kansas City the team that it became. I think it was between Dick Drago and me to go to the Reds. I think, for the organization, it was a good move. I didn't want to leave Kansas City ever. I tell people, though, that my claim to fame was that I was traded for Hal McRae."

—Roger Nelson

Roger, who was a huge hockey fan, stayed in Kansas City and worked for UPS for years and years.

The nickname Spider? He got that for his ability to steal passes while playing high school basketball.

Jorge Orta

Right or wrong, most people likely will remember Jorge Orta as the central figure in that controversial play at first in Game 6 of the 1985 World Series.

Jorge was a good offensive player with a quick, short swing. Defensively, there never was a position that he could play or that the Royals felt comfortable with him playing.

One of the great lines about Orta was when he was with the White Sox. He came up as a second baseman, but it was always risky putting him anywhere defensively. Harry Caray was broadcasting the game for the White Sox. Anyone who listened to Harry knows that he took losses and bad plays personally. As the story goes, the White Sox were playing the Texas Rangers at old Comiskey Park on a Saturday afternoon, middle of summer, bright sun. Late in the game, it was tied and Texas had the bases loaded with two outs.

The batter hit a fairly routine popup to short right field, a pretty easy play for the second baseman. Orta went back for the play; with two outs, all the runners were rounding the bases. As the ball reached its apex, it was directly in the Chicago summer sun. Orta fought the sun, trying to find the baseball. He found it, but it was too late. At the last moment, the ball flicked off his fingertips and fell to the turf. Three runs scored, and the batter wound up at second base, giving Texas a three-run lead. Harry was just despondent. He said, "How in the world could a guy from Mexico lose a ball in the sun?"

So when I think of Jorge Orta, I think of the World Series and the guy from Mexico losing the ball in the sun. But I guess I orta think that way, huh?

Marty Pattin

I first encountered Marty Pattin when we were in high school. He grew up in the Charleston, Illinois, area, and I grew up in Bloomington. We played against each other all through high school, in American Legion ball every summer, and in college. Marty played at Eastern Illinois, and I played at Illinois Wesleyan.

Marty was a hard thrower. He came right over the top with a lot of high fastballs and an occasional little breaking ball. At that time, though, he was one of the better pitchers in the state. We had a memorable college game against him at Illinois Wesleyan on a cold early April day. It was one of those raw days with snow flurries.

I came to bat with a guy on first and nobody out. Coach wanted me to bunt. So I laid one down and sprinted toward first. Marty came chugging down, picked up the ball and rocketed it to first base. It hit me in the back of the batting helmet, deflecting without serious injury all the way into the right field corner. Our runner who was on first scored, which turned out to be the only run of the game. Marty and I have kidded about that over the years. He always says, "If I knew that was you, I would have thrown the ball harder."

When I got to the big leagues in 1969, Marty was with the Seattle Pilots. He then went to Boston, where we'd hook up and go to dinner whenever the Royals were there.

Marty's been an acquaintance and a friend of mine for a long, long time. So it was a lot of fun when he came to the Royals.

Pitching, Marty never had a bad arm. He could eat up innings, pitching as a starter, in middle relief, or short relief late in the game. Marty's not an imposing guy physically by any stretch, but he was one of those lucky guys who never really had to fight many injuries.

The Rubber Duck

The only thing Marty ever fought was his weight. He loved to eat. There are many stories that won't be retold about how Marty, who's known as the "Duck" because of his uncanny Donald Duck impression, irritated some poor waitress because he tried to order in duck.

A toast to the "Duck." Fred White (right) and I celebrating with Marty Pattin after the Duck got his 100th win in Minnesota, September 9, 1977.
Photo courtesy of Denny Matthews

To try to combat his weight, he used to wear a rubber warmup suit and run in the outfield before games. We were in Minnesota—in the Twins' old stadium—and it was real hot and humid. Marty was running in the outfield, and he became dehydrated and collapsed. It was a scary situation, because, obviously, it wasn't known at that time that he was dehydrated. An ambulance came and rushed him to the hospital. The players were absolutely stunned by it.

Unfortunately, it was before the first game of a doubleheader. I don't remember the outcome, but I do remember that everyone was worried about Marty during that first game. Everybody went trooping back to the clubhouse between games to get a few minutes of rest and get something to eat and drink. They also wanted to call the hospital and check on Marty. Well, no need for that. When the guys got to the clubhouse, there was ol' Duck, putting a dent in the food spread. Evidently, he recovered nicely from his dehydration.

Lord of the Dance He's Not

Fred White and I found this Irish bar in Chicago called the Emerald Isle. They had a live Irish band that started playing around 9:00 at night. It was a cool place. Plus, it was only four or five blocks from our hotel near Rush Street.

This one particular trip, we had a day game with the White Sox on Saturday and then a doubleheader on Sunday. Fred and I told Marty, John "Duke" Wathan, George Brett and some of the other guys that we were going to the Emerald Isle around 7:30 that Saturday night. After a few of the guys had arrived, in came the Duck and the Duke.

Marty was scheduled to pitch the first game of Sunday's doubleheader, so Duke was Marty's chaperone or bodyguard for the night. Dukey needed to have Marty back to the hotel by 10:15 so he could get a good night's sleep.

We all were at the bar, sitting on those barstools with four metal legs, having a few drinks, when the band started. Then the place was jumping; it was a lively scene. Some girls in the bar came over and asked us to dance those Irish dances that none of us could do. This one cute girl came over and asked Marty to dance. Actually, she "encouraged" him. She grabbed him by the arm and pulled him toward the dance floor. She didn't realize that Marty's legs were wrapped around the barstool, like people often do. So here's Marty, tangled up in this barstool, being dragged by a woman while dragging this barstool behind. It was quite a sight. Finally, Marty freed himself from the barstool and got out there and did that goofy dance.

After the song, all the guys hooked back up at the bar. All of a sudden, Dukey looked at his watch and he said, "It's 10 after 10; come on, Duck, we gotta go back to the hotel." Against their wishes, Duke and Duck went back to the hotel.

About an hour later, at 11:30, we looked up and back in came Dukey and the Duck. Dukey had this goofy grin on his face and he said, "You know what, we were just having too much fun and we couldn't go to sleep."

At approximately 3:00 a.m., we went to this place kind of on the way back to the hotel for breakfast. It wasn't a nice place; just a little breakfast place. Marty's in his full Donald Duck routine. He was ordering breakfast in duck, and, as I mentioned, this was one time when the waitress was not amused. There's no telling, though, what time we got back to the hotel that night … er, should I say morning.

The next day, Marty was pitching in the first game of the twin bill, and it was hotter than blazes. It was stifling hot; you couldn't even draw a breath. Ducky's out there with sweat flying off him. But he pitched his little Duck butt off into the eighth inning, with the Royals leading 4-2. The Sox started to get a little rally going. They had two runners on when the batter ripped a shot into right center field for a single. One run scored, and the runner at first went to third. On the play, Ducky ran over to back up third base. When the play ended, he was sprawled out on the grass. He couldn't even raise his upper body. He got to his feet, and by that time, manager Whitey Herzog was on his way to the mound. He knew what was going on, so he had already called the bullpen. He gave Ducky a pat on the fanny and said with a grin, "Good job, Ducky, you are a gamer. You are a true gamer."

That was our night in Chicago.

Not Usually a Cutoff Play

Marty happened to be in the middle of one of the darndest plays I've ever seen in a game. It was in Milwaukee. Brett was playing third and Marty was pitching. The Brewers were in a bunting situation with a man at first. The batter laid down a great bunt along third. George came charging in, scooped it up in his bare hand and fired across his body, off balance, with his momentum going toward home. The rocket throw, however, looked perfect. Marty was about halfway between home plate and the pitcher's mound and in direct line with Brett. As soon as George unleashed the throw, Marty snapped up his glove and caught the throw. There wasn't much distance between Marty and George. So how Marty caught it, I don't know. Why he caught it, to this day he will not be able to tell you. It was a reactive, instinctive thing. He cut off what would have been a perfect throw to get the runner at first base.

All George could do was look at Marty as if to say, "What in the world was that!" Trying to describe that on the air was unbelievable. What do you say on a play when you expect the throw to get the runner, but in a split second the ball is snagged from the air? That will always be one of the darndest plays I've ever seen.

Lou Piniella

Lou Piniella joined the Royals at the end of spring training in 1969. He was traded for Steve Whitaker, an outfielder of whom the Yankees thought very highly, and John Gelnar.

Lou joined us on April 3 in Clearwater, Florida, about two hours before the final exhibition game. He played in the team's two weekend exhibition games against the Cardinals in Kansas City, and then he was in the starting lineup as a center fielder and leadoff man on opening day against the Twins.

Leading off against the Twins, Lou doubled, becoming the first batter in Royals history to double and the first, obviously, to get a hit. The next batter, Jerry Adair, got a base hit, driving in Lou for the club's first run (for Piniella) and RBI (for Adair).

In Lou's next three at-bats, he singled, flied out and walked. Then he drove in the winning run with two out in the 17th inning the next night against the Twins. Ten days later he collected the Royals' first triple and first two home runs at Municipal Stadium.

Yes, Lou had an incredible rookie season. Overall that first year, he hit .282 with 11 home runs and 68 RBIs, with 139 hits, 21 doubles and six triples in 135 games. During one stretch in the season, he hit in 24 of 26 games. What's more staggering is that he missed one weekend a month plus nearly two full weeks in August for military duty with the National Guard. (Since that was during the Vietnam War, many guys had to honor their military commitments.)

Lou also had a stretch of 60 consecutive errorless games. Defense might be the thing about Lou Piniella that a lot of people overlooked. I don't think I ever saw him drop a ball that he got his glove on, with the Royals or with other teams. His arm was average, but he definitely was sure-handed.

All of those numbers—offensively and defensively—helped Lou earn Rookie of the Year honors that season, the first rookie award for Kansas City major-leaguers. Dick Howser with the A's in 1961 and pitcher Jim Nash in 1966 had been the closest previously to winning one of the two rookie awards given by *The Sporting News.*

The Mad Hatter

Lou was a very outgoing, fun guy to be around, but he was very volatile. His temper was legendary.

When the Royals started, they wore the button-down jersey tops. Every once in a while, Lou would get so frustrated when making an out that after he'd throw his bat and helmet, he didn't have anything left, so he would grab his jersey top by the collar and pull on it as hard as he could. Of course, all of the buttons would go rocketing off his uniform jersey. Buttons were flying everywhere; guys were ducking.

Then we went to the double-knit pullovers. No buttons. Well, even then, Lou occasionally reverted to old form. One game when he hit into a double play—after the batting helmet and bat were tossed—he grabbed his jersey. Lou, who was really frustrated by this point, just kept pulling and pulling, but to no avail.

Can We Get a Plumber Down Here?

At Municipal Stadium, once you went down into the dugout near the home plate end, you'd go down three more steps, and to your left was a phone booth-sized room that accommodated the toilet and a wash basin. They say that after Lou hit into a double play one game, he was so livid that he went down those extra steps, where people couldn't see him, took his batting helmet, slammed it into the toilet bowl and flushed it.

Obviously the batting helmet wouldn't go down the hole, so it kept spinning in the stool. That only infuriated him more, so he grabbed his bat and started to plunge the helmet down. Shoot, that didn't work either. So, they say, he yanked the batting helmet out of the john, walked out and fired that poor helmet down the runway toward the clubhouse.

It was funny because a lot of times people wanted to see what kind of fit Lou was going to throw after making an out. We could see partially into the dugout, but since Lou sometimes would get out of sight, I'd watch the players on the bench. So many times the guys would sit there looking at the field, and then when Lou got down into the dugout, you'd see everybody's head turn to the left to see what the explosion was going to be.

One-Eyed Lou

We were playing a Saturday afternoon game at Municipal on a sunny, hot day. Lou hit into an inning-ending double play. As expected, he rounded first base after the out, cussing and kicking the dirt and grass to vent his frustration. Freddie Patek brought out Lou's glove with his sunglasses inside. Lou grabbed the glove and sunglasses and stalked out to left field still thinking about grounding into the double play. It was obvious he was still cussing himself out.

Lou took his hat and jammed it onto his head crooked. Then he took his sunglasses and fired them into left field ahead of him and kept walking out there. Then the glove went hurtling toward left. (The fans were getting a big kick out of it.) Lou got out there, picked up the glasses, put them on his head, and then grabbed his glove.

The second batter up in the inning hit a high, but routine, fly ball into the left field sun. Well, what Lou hadn't realized was that when he threw his glasses on the ground, one of the lenses popped out. So when he flipped down the glasses for this fly ball, Lou's blinded in one eye from the light of the sun. With one lens in and one lens out, Lou started spinning around wildly in a circle, trying to get an angle on the ball. He just kept spinning around like a top, out of control. But somehow, in some miraculous way, he caught the ball.

Things like that seemed to happen to Lou all the time. Some of the stuff that he did was hilarious. If Lou was an average or below average player, the instances might not be as funny (or certainly not things one would mention in a book). But Lou was a very good player, probably the team's first star.

Batting for Perfection

Lou worked very hard on his hitting. Often he would be in left field, working on his stance or his swing. He also got to the park early each day for batting practice. Succeeding and being the best hitter he could be was important to him.

To get to the dugout from the press box at Municipal, you had to walk down the steps in the lower level of seats and then go through a gate onto the field. There wasn't an elevator or steps that went from the press box to the field level, as we have today at Kauffman Stadium. Buddy Blattner was going down to the field to do an interview and talk to some players before a game. It was about 3:30 in the afternoon, when the stadium still was quiet because fans weren't there yet. The only noise came from players chatting and taking batting practice.

As Buddy got close to the field, a bat came flying halfway up the screen. Buddy was shocked, to say the least. About that time, Lou shouts out, "This fu--ing game is too tough!" Lou was hitting about .339 at the time, saying how the game is too tough. Buddy was telling me the story in the booth and said, "When I played, if we were hitting .339, we were pretty happy with that." Things haven't changed much today.

Lou, his wife Anita, and their kids lived in a nice house on Lee Boulevard, just off of 95th street. One night, about 3:30, Anita woke up to a light coming out of the cracked bathroom door. She said Lou was standing in the bathroom, totally naked, with a bat in his hands, checking out his batting stance in the mirror. That's not a pretty image, but that was Lou.

Darrell Porter

"Double-Barrel" Darrell Porter brought a high-intensity attitude and a winning attitude to the Royals. Whitey Herzog loved him. Darrell was a winner in every respect. He was really good in the clutch and always had a high on-base percentage. He always drew a lot of walks, scored a lot of runs. Overall, he just had as good a feel of the game of baseball—the little things everybody talks about and hardly anybody does much about.

He was probably in the top four or five base runners the Royals have ever had. Not base stealers—he wasn't fast—but one of the best base runners ever for the Royals

Darrell was hard-nosed, tough and highly competitive.

Right around the players' strike in 1994, the Royals played a Wednesday night game, had an off day on Thursday and then a home game on Friday, which didn't happen because of the strike. On that Thursday at Kauffman Stadium, there was a Royals/celebrity softball game for the RBI (Reviving Baseball in the Inner City) Program in Kansas City.

It was Royals alumni, front office, whoever wanted to get in on the game, against the Chiefs/celebrities. There were a bunch of Chiefs players, a couple wrestlers and some of the radio-TV types from town against our team. There were about 9,000 people there.

Fred White was our manager. Darrell caught, I played second and Freddie Patek played short. The Piggly Wiggly grocery store mascot was there. (Piggly Wiggly was one of the sponsors.)

Darrell Porter and I second-guess Fred White's decision to use Piggly Wiggly as a pinch runner in the benefit softball game during the players' strike in 1994.
Photo courtesy of Denny Matthews

We were down a run late in the game. We had a runner on base, and Fred thought it would be a cute idea to have Piggly Wiggly go to first base as a pinch runner. Darrell, Fred and I were near the end of the dugout. When we got the runner on, Fred said to Piggly Wiggly, "You go to first base and pinch run." Darrell all of a sudden realized what was going on, and he was aghast. Darrell, in his Oklahoma accent, turned to Fred and said, "Fred, you can't use Piggly Wiggly as our pinch runner. Don't you realize that Piggly Wiggly is the tying run?"

The statement alone is funny, but coming out of Darrell Porter's mouth made it even funnier. He just did not want Piggly Wiggly at first base representing the tying run late in the game. So we didn't use Piggly Wiggly as the tying run, and we still eventually won the game. That little incident, though, shows you, even in a celebrity charity softball game, how competitive Darrell Porter was and how his mind worked.

Darrell was interested in broadcasting. In fact, he came to spring training with us and sat in on a lot of games. He was trying to learn the rudiments of broadcasting. And, as with everything else he ever did, I'm sure, he really set his mind to it. He felt that if was attempting something, it should be done at 100 percent. He was almost a perfectionist. I'm sure some of the things in his life that he didn't accomplish, at least in his mind, really bothered him.

But Darrell was a sweetheart of a guy, and I always liked him and admired him for what he was and how he competed. He was with us in the booth a couple days before he died in 2002. We went to New York at the start of a road trip, and that's where we heard about it. He'll always be missed.

Jamie Quirk

Jamie Quirk, who grew up in California, turned down scholarship offers from Notre Dame and a few other colleges to play football. Then the Royals drafted him and signed him. Jamie had the best disposition of everybody who has ever played for us. He is always friendly, always has something nice to say.

The thing about James as a player was that there never was one position defensively that was his spot. Hitting wasn't the issue, because he always could swing the bat pretty well. But he never had a position. Then Whitey made him a catcher and prolonged his career.

Since his playing career has ended, Jamie has done a little bit of everything. I think eventually he wants to manage in the big leagues, which would be great. He's had a lot of good coaching experience, and he knows the game.

Three's Company

Jamie, George Brett and I went to Hawaii together in November, 1974. It was one of those "Royals fans, join George Brett, Jamie Quirk and Denny Matthews in Hawaii," fan-type trips. None of us was married at the time, so Hawaii for about 10 days was not a bad gig. We took a bunch of pictures that trip, which I still have somewhere. We had a blast. We followed a pretty stringent schedule during the day, but then about 7:30 at night, the three "co-hosts" would sneak away for the rest of the night. It was quite a trip.

George Brett (left), Jamie Quirk and I, in 1978, were still trying to recover from our Hawaii trip four years earlier. We were the social directors for 80 eager Royals tourists. How could you not want to follow any of these three?

Photo courtesy of Denny Matthews

Fred Rico

On the field, Fred Rico, who was with the Royals in 1969, didn't make a major contribution. Off the field, however, he was huge. In June of 1970, Rico was traded to the St. Louis Cardinals for Cookie Rojas. That certainly was one of the best early trades that the organization made. For that alone, he deserves a note in Royals history.

Rey Sanchez

I would say that Rey Sanchez, who was with the Royals during 1999-2001, was the steadiest shortstop that the Royals have ever had. He made every routine play because his footwork was better than any shortstop the Royals have had. His footwork was almost perfect.

People tried to say that he was good because he never got any bad hops. Well, he didn't get many bad hops because his footwork put him in position where he was dictating the hop that he would get. It's the old question: are you going to let the ball play you or are you going to play the ball? Rey played the ball. Obviously, it's subtle. People wouldn't go out to the park to watch Rey Sanchez's footwork at shortstop.

He could make the spectacular play, but the shortstop position is the one where you want to get every out that you should get. You want to make those routine plays. Baltimore's Mark Belanger did it beautifully. Detroit's Alan Trammell did it beautifully. Ozzie Smith did it beautifully (but threw in all the spectacular stuff, too). Rey was "Mr. Consistency."

Paul Schaal

Paul Schaal came from the Angels during the expansion draft with the 14th pick. He was the Royals' third baseman from 1969 until George Brett came along.

Paul had been hit in the ear by a pitch while he was with the Angels, and it caused some problems for him, particularly on defense. Paul was very smooth defensively. He wasn't a big power guy at the plate, but he was a good contact guy. His strength, though, was defense. Because of the inner ear problem from being hit by that pitch, when Paul looked up for popups, he would get dizzy and become disoriented at times. Everybody on the team knew that, so whenever there was a popup in short left field, or even foul just off third, our shortstop would make the play.

Most of the time that was Freddie Patek, who played off Paul better than any of the other shortstops. Freddie would go racing over from shortstop, and he would call Paul off every play that he could make.

After leaving baseball, Paul stayed in the Kansas City area. He opened a pizza shop, which is no longer around, and also became a successful chiropractor.

Richie Scheinblum

Richie Scheinblum, a switch hitter, played in the Central Illinois Collegiate League for Bloomington, my hometown. That's where I first met him. He hitchhiked from the East Coast to central Illinois to have a chance to try out with the Bloomington Bobcats with the CICL.

Richie, who played for the Royals in 1972 and 1974, was a funny guy with a goofy personality. Long before a game one day at Municipal Stadium, he was down by the railing, signing autographs. If you've ever been to a game early enough to see people get autographs, you know that once a player signs one, the people just swarm around the player. That's what happened this particular day with Richie.

I passed him at the railing on my way to interview someone for the pregame show. About 15 minutes later, I was headed back up to the booth, and there's Richie, in the same spot, diligently signing "Richie Scheinblum" for what seemed to be half the people in the stadium. I gave him a quizzical look, and he said, "Boy, I wish my name was Mel Ott."

That was a typical Richie Scheinblum comment.

George Scott

George Scott came to the Royals in June 1979, after a successful career with Boston. He was traded for Tom Poquette. When George got here, he pretty much had nothing left in the gas tank. His best years (and most of his post-best years) were behind him. Whitey Herzog mainly used George as a pinch hitter or as a fill-in at first base.

George's nickname was "Boomer," which obviously didn't have anything to do with his voice, because he certainly didn't talk like a

Boomer. (That is, unless sounds of a somewhat squeaky voice come to mind when you think about "Boomer.")

When George Scott got here, he wanted to wear No. 5, which had been his number with the Red Sox. Oftentimes when an older veteran goes to a new club, he'll get the same number, or, if someone already has that number, he might try to "buy" the number from whichever player currently has it. In the case of the Royals, there was a player here by the name of George already wearing No. 5.

For the life of Boomer, he couldn't figure out why he couldn't have No. 5. And he talked it up constantly ... on the bus, around the batting cage, in the clubhouse, you name it. In his squeaky voice he'd say, "I'm No. 5. I'm Boomer. I deserve respect." And other such lines.

As a part-timer, Boomer wasn't producing, but he still felt he deserved respect. We'd be on the road, for instance, and in his only at-

George Scott never did get his "earned" No. 5 while with the Royals ... but No. 0 seemed to be fitting. *Photo courtesy of the Kansas City Royals*

bat, he'd weakly ground the ball to third, or ground into an easy double play. But then he'd get on the bus and he'd start chirping about his number. "I'm No. 5. I'm Boomer. I've been in the big leagues for a long time. I deserve and I need respect."

This went on for three or four weeks after Boomer got here. Meanwhile, he's still hitting about .045, dinking little ground balls to the left side of the infield. He played first base one night and hit into a couple of double plays. I think he went zero for six in the game. We all were on the bus on our way back to the hotel, and here starts Boomer, still chirping about "No. 5."

Finally, somebody in the back of the bus snapped. The voice said, "Boomer, shut up. I'm sick and tired of listening to you talk about number 5. We are going to give you another number ... 6-4-3."

We didn't hear anything about No. 5 for the rest of the time George Scott was with us.

Rodney Scott

Rodney "Cool Breeze" Scott was the target for many of John Mayberry's jokes in the back of the bus. Rodney Scott thought he was a lot better than he was, but Big John always made sure he realized he wasn't that good.

Rodney carried the biggest boom box ever invented. Rodney was a little guy who could really run. So that boom box seemed to be about four times bigger than Rodney.

Mayberry had his normal seat at the back bench of the bus. It was a perfect place for him to hold court. Shortly after Rodney Scott joined the Royals in 1975, he wanted to sit at the back of the bus. Rodney alone was fine, but the boom box wasn't. Rodney got on the bus well ahead of Mayberry one time after a game in Minnesota, and he took one seat and the boom box took two more.

After almost everyone had gotten on the bus, here came Big John. He got halfway toward the back of the bus, looked toward his seat and saw Rodney Scott and his box. Big John just bellowed out, "Noooo, noooo, noooo, Breeze. Noooo." That's all he had to say because everybody knew what it meant. Most of all, Breeze understood, and he grabbed his box and scrambled out of the back seat.

Kevin Seitzer

Kevin Seitzer was a central Illinois boy, so you figured he'd be a great athlete and a good hitter. He was both. He broke in with a bang. He always gave off the impression that he worked hard to get the most out of his physical attributes. He was a good guy with a good sense of humor, funny one-liners and the kind of guy you enjoyed being around.

Kevin was the ultimate contact hitter. He could go to the opposite field or pull the ball, and he occasionally had power. Overall, though, he was just a tough out. He played hard, ran hard, and worked hard on his defense. Defense was not his forte, but he became a good third baseman. Again, he worked hard at it.

He really loved playing the game, which came out on the field. He was a player whom you could watch and feel that you were getting 100 percent out of him. I think the fans became attached to that. I think they sensed that he was giving them everything, instead of simply going through the motions.

Kevin came here in 1986, the year after the World Series, and provided a great spark for those first few years after the world championship.

Tony Solaita

Tony Solaita, who was from Samoa, was one of the biggest, strongest players in Royals history. Thank goodness he was a gentle, gentle guy. He was quiet and polite. At the time, Tony was the only Samoan baseball player in the big leagues.

Tony produced one of the longest and noisiest home runs in Royals history. We were in Detroit one night, and Tony absolutely crushed the ball. It was May 13, 1975, and Tony belted a Larren Lagrow pitch off the light tower in right center field. (That's the light tower that Reggie Jackson hit in his historic 1971 All-Star game poke.) Tony's shot was estimated to have traveled 550 feet, and it hit about 15 feet below where Jackson hit his. The noise that Tony's homer made was incredible; it was like a gunshot.

Tony hit another tape-measure homer off of Minnesota's Bert Blyleven at Royals Stadium. It was estimated at 450 feet into the right field bullpen.

In 1975, he hit 16 home runs, which was second on the club to Mayberry's 34, and had an outstanding home run ratio of one homer in every 14 at-bats. That ratio ranked us the best in the American League among players with 250 at-bats. Tony also had a .515 slugging percentage, which was second, also to Mayberry. At the time, he established the team record for runs scored on June 18 against the Angels, when he went three for three with a pair of homers and two walks, and he scored five runs.

Defensively, he made only two errors at first in 312 chances. He was a very smooth defensive player, too.

Tony Solaita died about 10 years ago. But what a sweetheart of a guy.

Bob Stinson

Bob Stinson was a catcher who loved going to the mound. He loved going out and talking to the pitcher. Whitey Herzog would scream at Stinson, "Get back behind the plate and just catch!" Still, Stinson would go trooping out there.

One night, we were ahead with Al Fitzmorris pitching at Royals Stadium, where you can sense thunderstorms gathering. The flags will start to blow hard, and you know that the storm is headed down I-70 from the west toward the ballpark. With the lead late in the game, Fitzy needed to get two more outs. Even Fitzy, who could be almost as slow as paint drying, was trying to hurry up.

All of a sudden, a blinding flash of lightning struck beyond the left field fence, followed by a clap of thunder that shook the stadium. We looked back down to the field and here came Stinson, in full catcher's gear, casually walking out to the mound. I think everybody in the stadium was screaming at him to get back to the plate. Certainly everyone in the Royals' dugout was screaming. Stinson got within about 10 feet of the mound, and Fitzy yelled at him, "Stins, get away from me with all those fu--ing buckles!" That was Bob Stinson.

Mike Sweeney

Mike Sweeney, who came up as a catcher, wasn't reaching his offensive potential in the games he worked behind the plate. So they had to make a move.

Sweeney is similar to other guys we've mentioned, such as Lonnie Smith and Kevin Seitzer, in that he gives his all every time he's on the field. He works very hard, offensively and defensively.

When the Royals first moved him to first base, it was obvious that he was uncomfortable there. Tony Muser helped him a ton in that regard. Then Lamar Johnson, who was the Royals' hitting coach, helped Mike a lot offensively. With Tony and Lamar, Sweeney started to become the type of player the Royals thought he'd be.

Mike's personality and character are beyond reproach. He's one of the true gentlemen ever to walk into the Royals clubhouse. The Royals have done an excellent job of culling out the potential bad guys and having quality people on their roster, but Mike's one of the top on that list. He endears himself to everybody. He's very genuine and sincere about helping people. Even though he's married, he's the type of person you'd want your daughter to marry.

(And he's a great guy to have on your team.)

Hoosier

We were together a few years ago on the Royals Caravan, which often stops at high schools. If we have time, guys will work out in the gym or play basketball or whatever. During one stop, a few of us were in a gym playing H-O-R-S-E, and it was almost time to leave. At the corner of the court there was an exit doorway.

I was shooting well this particular day, and so as we were getting ready to leave, my last shot was shot from that corner, slightly behind the basket. I launched a high, perfectly arched shot and yelled at Sweeney, "Five dollars if it goes in." I was through the door and out of the gym before the ball came down ... and swished. Ever since that shot, Sweeney has called me Hoosier. We'll always remember the five-dollar bet from the gym on the caravan. But I still haven't seen my five bucks!

Carl Taylor

Carl Taylor was a strange bird. He got so frustrated after a game in Baltimore, when he ended the game hitting into a double play or striking out, that he burned his uniform in the clubhouse. He decided that was it; he was quitting.

"Carl Taylor was a marginal catcher. I remember being on the bus one time and Taylor, who was Boog Powell's stepbrother, was having trouble finding a seat, so he yelled out, 'Why don't some of you people stand up and let a real ballplayer sit down?' A voice replied, 'Good idea, Carl, but you're already standing.'"

—*Fred White*

Yep, Taylor was wound pretty tight. He was very bizarre.

Jerry Terrell

Jerry Terrell was a versatile player and a hard worker. Indeed, he pitched in a blowout game at Kauffman Stadium against New York and recorded three outs on three pitches. You can't do any better than that. That's a perfect inning if there ever was one. Jerry and his family still live in Kansas City. He is a true gentleman.

George Throop

George Throop was a tall (six-feet-seven), skinny pitcher. One night before a game he was discovered hanging from a clubhouse doorway by his feet. Someone had convinced George that if he would hang upside down, wearing these boots, his circulation would improve and he'd gain great amounts of energy. George bought into the idea and would throw on the boots and hang upside down periodically. I'm still not sure how he got into that contraption, or out of it for that matter.

John Wathan

John Wathan does the best John Wayne imitation; hence the nickname "The Duke." Whitey Herzog called Duke his "cornfield player," even though Dukey may never have set foot on a farm. But Whitey knew that he could put Dukey anywhere defensively, which he did, pretty much.

Wathan was not considered a "hot" prospect in the Royals organization in any of the years that he was moving up in the system. In fact, each year on his evaluation as a player, he was labeled NP (No Prospect). But he kept working and improving to the point where he made the big leagues and became a solid big-league player. He made himself a major league baseball player, and you have to admire him for that.

When Duke first started, he wasn't that fast, he didn't have a great arm, and he didn't have a lot of power. Actually, sportswriter Mike McKenzie had one of the great lines about Wathan's power when they had a little dinner honoring Duke at his retirement.

McKenzie said, "John, you had the perfect nickname. Everybody knows about your John Wayne imitations, but that's not the reason why your nickname is perfect. It's because when you hit the ball, you hit those little bloopers out into right field, and the sound that your bat made … duke … duke … duke." He got a lot of grief about that.

But he was a good offensive player. He was a good contact guy, a perfect hit-and-run batter, and he stole bases. In fact, in 1982, in a game against Texas, he set the single-season record for stolen bases by a catcher.

"I stole third off of Frank Tanana in Arlington to break the record. However, I think the grounds crew assumed I'd be stealing second if I broke the record. So, thinking they'd be giving me second base, they put an old base there and a brand new base at third. They couldn't get the new base out of the ground. It took them forever to get it out. It was kind of embarrassing, standing there while they worked to get it out. Finally, they did. That's a game I'll never forget. That base is now a part of a barstool at my house."

—John Wathan

Duke was able to start stealing more bases when he learned how to take a walking lead. He was the master of that. He had a great knack for continuing to move on his leadoff, so he had the momentum going when he wanted to steal.

He has done about everything possible in the Royals organization: player, coach, manager, broadcaster, and now scout.

Jim Wohlford

Jim Wohlford was one of Steve Mingori's targets. Actually, come to think of it, Wolfy was a target for most of the guys. Wolfy was an unwittingly funny guy. But he always took other people's ribbings in good humor. Wohlford was in that left field platoon situation with Tom Poquette. Wolfy was a small guy, a small outfielder not possessing much power. However, he was a good contact hitter, and he could run.

Wohlford loved Detroit outfielder Al Kaline. In fact, Wolfy wore No. 6 with the Royals in honor of his Tiger hero.

Deadwood

One year during spring training, before he had made the big-league roster, Wohlford put himself in an awkward situation. Of course, in early spring training there are many guys who aren't going to make the club. He used to say to me from time to time, "Denny, Jim Wohlford can hit." "Yeah, yeah, I know, Wolfy, you can hit." But this one day in Fort Myers, he was in the group that was taking batting practice. There must have been eight or 10 guys in his group, which means each player's only getting five or six swings and maybe a bunt. In that situation, it was tough for everyone to get good work.

I was standing next to the batting cage and Wolfy got his five or six hacks, and he came out of the batting cage. I could tell he was a little bit irritated. (Keep in mind, Jim Wohlford was one of the nicest guys on the team. I never heard him say a bad thing about anyone.) He said, "Boy, I can't wait until we get some of the deadwood out of here," meaning some of the minor league guys, "so we can get some more swings."

Sure enough, the next morning, some of that "deadwood" was on the bus headed to the minor league camp at Sarasota ... including Jim Wohlford.

Beer, Broads, Baseball and the Bible

Before the new stadium was built in Arlington, Texas, that was a great place to be (I'll say sarcastically) after games. There were a couple motels, the ballpark, Six Flags amusement park, a couple of bars and a Steak and Ale next to the motel where we stayed.

The Steak and Ale was the place to be. Besides the steak and ale, the restaurant had plenty of girls and a band. I always said you could get discovered at the Steak and Ale by falling out the door—it was just one of those places where the women outnumbered the guys.

Fred White and I—and most of the team—were in there one night after a game; it's lively, there's dancing. Wolfy came up to the bar where Fred and I were talking to a couple guys, and he squeezed in between us and ordered a beer. Wolfy had been having problems offensively, he wasn't saying much, and he wasn't too involved in the conversation. When things got a little bit quiet, he looked at Fred and I and said, "Guys, will you pray with me?"

Understandably, the request threw most of us off base. Not that praying is a bad thing, but we were in a bar, after all. Fred looked at him and said, "Well, Wolfy, I'm not sure this is the place."

Wolfy replied, "I really, really have to get rid of this slump. Won't you please pray with me?"

Fred thought for a second before saying, "How about if I just buy you another beer?"

The Bears Hibernate on the Weekend

I remember one Sunday morning at Fenway Park in Boston, a few hours before the game, there were a few guys in the dugout, including Lou Piniella. Lou was involved in the stock market. He always talked about it and enjoyed it a lot, and Wohlford knew that.

Wolfy came out of the tunnel and into the dugout. Jim wanted to be in conversations, say something intelligent, but it was sometimes awkward. When he came into the dugout he said, "Hey Lou, how are you doing today? How's the stock market doing today?"

Lou just gave him this dumbfounded look and said, "Wolfy, it's Sunday morning. The stock market hasn't been open since Friday afternoon." Then Lou just shook his head and walked away.

Ken Wright

Ken Wright was a big, big, big guy. He was about six foot four and weighed around 270 pounds. His weight was the killer. He had a great arm for a power pitcher, but he had trouble controlling his weight. His dad owned a bakery, which didn't help. Ken's nickname was "Burger" for obvious reasons. During the off season, Burger worked in the family bakery. Come spring training, there wasn't any doubt where he had been working in the winter.

For part of one season, Burger and Piniella roomed together. As Lou tells the story, they got back to the hotel after a game in Baltimore around 11:30. There was a crummy all-night burger stand right across from the hotel. This place had the small burgers like White Castle or Krystal. So you had to get at least three or four to feel as if you'd eaten something.

When Lou and Burger got back to the room, they were hungry. Lou said, "I'll go across the street and get us some burgers." Lou went out and got 12 of those little hamburgers and took them back to the room. He set them on the nightstand between the beds and went into the bathroom real quick. When he came out, the burgers were all gone.

Lou recently told me the story and he said, "I wasn't in the bathroom that long. But I came back, and I started rooting around in the sack to get three or four burgers for myself. I was getting nothing but air. Burger had consumed the burgers in record time!" I asked Lou if he went back across to get some for himself. He said, "I don't remember; I was so mad."

Jim York

Jim York was a good relief pitcher whom we traded to Houston to get John Mayberry.

In Chicago, York, a big good-looking guy, and I hooked up with a couple TWA flight attendants that we knew. After the Saturday afternoon game, we caught up with our friends, had dinner and then went back to their apartment on the North Side. One thing led to another, and it got late, extremely late, as in about 7:30 Sunday morning. We still had to get back to the Executive House Hotel, where we were staying, pack our bags and catch the bus at 10:00 to head to the ballpark.

While we were in the cab nearing the hotel I told Yorkie, "You know, we probably should not go through the lobby." I knew of another door that would take us through the dining room area of the hotel and then right to the elevators. We could go zipping upstairs, bypassing the lobby, thereby missing manager Bob Lemon and anyone else we didn't really need to see, even though it was early enough that most baseball people wouldn't be awake yet.

Not that it would have been too big a deal to see Lem, considering he was an old-school baseball guy, and someone who, as a player, was

Jim York drew the ire of manager Bob Lemon because of me ... or maybe I drew the ire of Lemon because of York. I'm not sure but we certainly pulled a memorable all-nighter in Chicago. *Photo courtesy of the Kansas City Royals*

always willing to have a drink with you. His nickname for everyone was "Meat." Now that's an old-school baseball guy.

Anyway, as planned, we went through the dining room, and everything was cool. If you took this to Las Vegas, I don't know what the odds would have been, but when the doors opened to one of those elevators, there was Bob Lemon, bigger than life. He was coming down to get his paper and have breakfast. It was quite obvious that we had not been in the dining room having breakfast.

Yorkie was just paralyzed. Lem, who always had a rough expression on his face, looked at York, looked at me and he got a little twinkle in his eye. The best that Yorkie could do was say, "Hey, Skip, try the pancakes. They're great." Lem looked at him and said, "Yeah, right, Meat."

And with that he got off the elevator, we got on and that was the end of it. I don't think Lemon ever said a word to Yorkie, and I know he never said anything to me.

Chapter
7
PARTNERS IN CRIME

I have been one lucky broadcaster, because in 35 years I've had only three radio partners and only two producers/engineers. We obviously spend quite a bit of time together in the booth, at home and on the road.

The guys who have helped us get on the air and stay on the air each game for 35 years, our producer/engineers, were the late Ed Shepherd and currently Don Free. You hear their names during each broadcast. Each a unique individual, the producer/engineer often goes beyond the call of duty to help ensure a great broadcast.

Shep was pretty laid back, while Don is pretty high-tempo. Both very competent, they could fix anything.

Ed Shepherd

Ed Shepherd, who worked on the Kansas City A's broadcasts, was stocky, with his shirt tail always hanging out. His clothes were ill-fitting and out of style, which I think he kind of liked. But he was one of the most well-rounded people I've ever met. He died in 1992. He is missed.

Baby, It's Cold Outside

Shep knew every piano bar in every city and every bartender in those bars. We were in Minneapolis late in the season, and Shep was in the Ivanhoe, a piano bar. There was a guy a couple seats away. Shep started talking to the guy and found out that he had a fishing camp about 500 miles north of there, in Canada. People went to this place

Ed Shepherd leading me through another pregame show, this time with Royals manager Bob Lemon in 1970. *Photo courtesy of Denny Matthews*

during the summer months to fish. The guy told Shep that they try to stay open from May until the first part of September. Shep said, "Well, what brings you to Minneapolis?"

"It gets so cold up there that I come south for the winter to stay warm."

Don't Ask, Don't Tell

Whenever we got to a town, regardless of when we arrived, Shep's "job" was to go out and get beer, chips, and snacks for Bud Blattner's room. Most of the time there would be a get-together in Bud's room; sometimes it would be in Shep's room.

We got into Cleveland one night about 2:00 a.m., and nothing was stirring. Regardless, at 2:00 a.m., here goes Shep for his task. He came back about 20 minutes later, with beer and snacks. Where he went and how he knew any place was open, or what place was open, nobody knew. And we never asked.

One night the get-together was in Shep's room. When I went into the bathroom, Shep had all sorts of stuff on the counter. A pomegranate—a tropical reddish fruit—was sticking out of his shaving kit. Now I'm sure there was a good reason for having it, but, much like the snacks in Cleveland, we never asked him. After all, how many people carry a pomegranate in their shaving kit?

That was so typical of Ed Shepherd.

Thomas Edison Would Be Proud

Every year in early February, we would convene at Royals Stadium to record commercials and promos for all the stations on the network. We would spend the whole morning doing that. About four hours later, we would be done and Shep would stop his tape recorder.

One time when we were doing that, Bob Stiegler, the top salesman for the Royals Radio Network, said after we finished, "Isn't it nice with the technology now how easy it is to do this? Think how complicated this was 20 or 30 years ago." Bob then asked Shep how he used to record in the early days.

Shep said, "We would take a disk, like a record, and put a needle in hot wax. That would produce some shavings of wax, which we take sometimes and make into a ball."

He then walked over to his sport coat and pulled out a ball of record wax shavings. We were stunned. I'm pretty confident in making this statement: not another person in the entire city had a ball of record wax shavings in his sport coat pocket on that particular morning!

He Should Have Charged Admission

Ed Shepherd's house was like a museum. In his basement sat the piano on which Count Basie learned to play. He also had a key-making machine down there. When his dad retired, he thought he might want to stay busy, so Ed bought him a key-making machine.

Shep also had other artifacts and pictures. We came to this picture that looked as if it had been taken in the late 1800s. Shep pointed to a guy and said that it was his wife's great-great grandfather. He said, "They were all musicians. They're all dead now." You don't say.

Don Free

Don Free, who has been our producer-engineer since 1986, really enjoys his work. He takes care of the scoreboard, the scores and updates

Don Free hard at work. *Photo courtesy of Denny Matthews*

of other games you hear during a Royals broadcast. But he really does much more.

Don, who commutes to Kansas City from Topeka, arrives at the stadium around 2:00 p.m. and sometimes doesn't leave until close to 2:00 a.m. Then he drives to Topeka, sleeps for a few hours, spends the morning with his wife and dog or the grandkids, and then turns around and heads back to Kauffman Stadium. His dedication is amazing.

Many of the guys call him "World B." after the former NBA player World B. Free, but they also call on him to fix any electronic equipment. It's common for guys to bring things up to the booth before a game and ask Don if he can fix it. Usually, he can. Actually if Don can't repair it, chances are that it's beyond repair. I could find an old tape recorder that hasn't worked in 20 years, take it to Don, and he could fix it.

You name it, Don can do it. He has tremendous dedication to his job and putting the best possible broadcast on the air.

Buddy Blattner

Buddy Blattner, the Royals' first "voice" and my mentor, was very much a technician as a broadcaster. He played the game, so he had a good feel for what was happening on the field, and he could relay that to the listener with a great voice. We had that old-school type of broadcast, where the guy calling the play-by-play is the guy. It was mostly a one-voice production.

One of the first things Bud said to me was to do the game my own way and not to try to be like anyone else. "If it is my innings, feel free to add whatever you want. I want you to develop your own style," he said. "I'm not going to crowd you." I adopted the philosophy with Fred White and Ryan Lefebvre.

Bud was very businesslike, but he always had fun. The only rule he had was that we couldn't drink any adult beverages before or during a game. We could after, but not before. That was his only "rule."

He was great to me. He knew everybody, and he made sure he introduced me to everyone. He would always steer me toward the guys who were good to interview, which was helpful.

Bud was a good storyteller. He announced the Game of the Week, a national broadcast, with Dizzy Dean, and was excellent. However, I never heard Bud call a baseball game until we started working together with the Royals.

My first partner and mentor was Buddy Blattner. This photo was taken at the old stadium. *Photo courtesy of Denny Matthews*

I remember in high school listening to Bud on KMOX, calling St. Louis Hawks games. He may have been the best pro basketball announcer ever. He was terrific. He had a nickname for every player, and he had some great sayings.

One of my favorite sayings, when there was a foul on a play and Bud was waiting to see who committed it, he'd say, "A foul has been called under the basket … and they are walking the wrong way," meaning the foul was on the Hawks. I always thought that was a cool expression.

Fred White

Fred White was working in Topeka when he joined Buddy and me as a third man. We were starting to broadcast games on television, so we were going to have a three-man rotation. It also was great to have Fred there a couple years before Bud retired. When Bud did leave, I took over his seat, and Fred took over my spot.

Fred and I discovered quite early that we came from the same part of the country, central Illinois, so we had that in common. He was easy to work with. His personality is pretty laid back. The transition for me was going from the No. 2 guy to replacing a guy who had done national

My partner for 25 years, Fred White. Our mutual central Illinois backgrounds helped us click immediately. *Photo courtesy of Denny Matthews*

work. Plus, I knew the ball club was going to be pretty good, so we had that pressure.

Fred had not done a lot of baseball at that point, so he was trying to establish himself. We were just trying to prop each other up. I think it worked out pretty well. I guess the fact that we spent 25 years together would suggest that.

Neither one of us was on a huge ego trip, so we worked well together. We would get off on tangents during the game. Some people enjoyed that; others didn't like it. We walked a fine line in that area.

We had a lot fun talking about things that didn't have anything to do with the game, but that were humorous. A brawl broke out next to the booth in Chicago at Comiskey Park. Bill Veeck, a marketing genius but a tough son of a gun who owned the White Sox then, opened the door from the press box to the area where the fight was happening and wanted to break it up. He came back into the booth with a bloody lip. And the fight had stopped. That gave Fred and me some material.

Fred has a good sense of humor, and he can take something that he sees in the stands or on the field and make it funny. A three-hour game has only 18 to 20 minutes of actual action, which leaves a lot of time to talk about other stuff.

25 Years and Gone Without an Explanation

After we had spent 175-200 games together each season for 25 years, Fred was fired following the 1998 season. Right after the season, we each had meetings scheduled with the folks at Entercom, the group that held the Royals' Radio rights at that time.

Fred and I were going to play golf at Indian Hills in the Kansas City area after our meetings. Fred's was the previous afternoon, and mine was the morning we played golf. My meeting, as usual, was brief and to the point. We got our deal done, and away I went to play golf with Fred.

Arriving at the golf course, assuming everything would be the same in the 1999 season as it had been the previous 25 years, I casually asked Fred how his meeting went. He said, "Not very well. They let me go." I was floored. I had no idea. All I could ask was why. Needless to say, that was the topic of conversation for the round of golf and for the rest of the day.

Apparently they told him it was a monetary thing; they were strapped for cash. Regardless, it was startling news. It was a move that shocked Royals fans as much as any "blockbuster" trade or signing that the Royals made on the field.

Ironically, after a couple seasons away, Fred returned to the Royals. He oversees the Royals Alumni group and is helping build the radio and TV networks. He also fills in for me during about 20 broadcasts each season.

It was good for Fred to rejoin the team in the alumni function. He has done a great job reconnecting with the alumni and bringing them back to the ballpark. Fred was so popular with players and fans that he was a good fit for the alumni. Nowadays there are a lot of the former players at the stadium.

Fred's filling in for me the past three years has given me the opportunity to recharge my battery and has been good for Fred as well.

When you think about it, his tenure with the club is nearly as long as anyone else's in the organization. I hate that things didn't work out for us to continue working together on the radio, but it's good to see Fred back at the stadium.

Ryan Lefebvre

My personality does not lend itself to change. I am not comfortable with it. So I wasn't eager to go out and help find a replacement for Fred.

I listened to a lot of the audition tapes. We came down to 12 or 15, of which I thought three were good. Ryan's was one of those. It's obvious when listening to him that he played the game and he does his homework.

When Ryan first came to Kansas City, we got together at a barbecue place in Martin City. As we talked, we were struck with the similarities in our backgrounds.

His dad was a good major league player and manager, and my dad was an All-American second baseman in college before receiving offers from Cincinnati and the White Sox. Ryan and I both played in college. We both were broadcasting major league games in our mid-20s, which is highly unusual. We just seemed to have a good connection early.

Ryan is easy to work with. He's not intense or uptight. He has a lot in common with the players. It's funny, when I started, Buddy had much in common with the general managers, managers, and coaches, and I had more in common with the players. As I have gotten older, I've associated more with the general managers, managers and coaches, while

Ryan associates with the players. As he goes on, he will have less in common with the players and more with the managers and coaches.

I think Ryan did an excellent job of handling the pressure of taking over for Fred. For obvious reasons, Fred's firing was not popular, and fans were skeptical of Ryan, but he's handled everything very well. There is always an awkward transition period for the new guy. There was an uncomfortable period when I succeeded Buddy, and there was an awkward period when Ryan succeeded Fred. It just takes a while for the new person to feel comfortable. It takes time for the listeners to feel comfortable. It just takes time, but it has worked out very well.

That's a Wrap

Since I've done both radio and TV with the Royals, I've had a chance to work with some other great broadcasters, including former players Steve Busby, Paul Splittorff and John Wathan, plus Denny Trease and Bob Davis. Each of these guys, and the others who have been on radio and TV for the Royals, have been fun to work with and have made this job even more enjoyable.

Indeed, what a charmed life this has been.

Ryan Lefebvre has a good family baseball background. He should be a solid big-league announcer for many years to come. *Photo courtesy of the Kansas City Royals*

Denny Matthews (right) has been with the Kansas City Royals as a radio announcer since the club's first season, 1969. He teamed with Buddy Blattner until 1975, and then became the team's number-one announcer, working for 25 years with Fred White. He is one of a few broadcasters in baseball that has broadcast exclusively for the same team, without interruption, in five different decades. And he's one of only six announcers in Major League history to spend his entire career with one team, while logging at least 35 consecutive seasons. Matthews, who has worked games also for the CBS Radio Network, was inducted into the Royals Hall of Fame in 2004, and into the Missouri Sports Hall of Fame in 2005. Matthews, a 1966 graduate of Illinois Wesleyan, lettered in baseball and football for three years, and finished eighth in the nation in the NAIA for pass receiving in 1965. In 1999, along with Fred White and Matt Fulks, Matthews co-authored "Play by Play: 25 Years of Royals on Radio." Matthews is an avid golfer and hockey player. He resides in the Kansas City area.

Matt Fulks (left) started his journalism career while attending Lipscomb University in Nashville, Tennessee, after his baseball career was cut short by a lack of ability. Since then he has worked in every form of the media, and now spends his time as a freelance writer, editor, and broadcaster. He is a regular contributor to various publications, including *The Kansas City Star* newspaper and the *Royals Gameday* magazine. He is the author/co-author of eight other books, including *Behind the Stats: Tennessee's Coaching Legends*, *The Road to Canton*, co-authored with NFL Hall of Fame running back Marcus Allen, and *Good as Gold: Techniques for Fundamental Baseball*, with Royals legend Frank White. Fulks, who has turned to a life of cycling and hockey, resides in the Kansas City area with his wife, Libby, their children, Helen, Charlie and Aaron, and their Doberman retriever.